The Novels of Daya Dissanayake

Critical Expositions

The Novels of Daya Dissanayake

Critical Expositions

Editor

P.V. LAXMIPRASAD

AUTHORSPRESS

Worldwide Circulation through Authorspress Global Network
First Published in 2022
by
Authorspress
Q-2A Hauz Khas Enclave, New Delhi-110 016 (India)
Phone: (0) 9818049852
E-mail: authorspressgroup@gmail.com
Website: www.authorspressbooks.com

The Novels of Daya Dissanayake: Critical Expositions
ISBN 978-93-5529-140-0

Printed in India at Thomson Press (India) Limited

Biography of Daya Dissanayake

Daya Dissanayake was born in Galle, Sri Lanka in March of 1947. His full name is Dayananda Dissanayake and he is one of the five siblings born to parents Albert Dissanayake and Agnus Wavala Panditha. When he was fourteen years old, Dissanayake's father died. From then he was raised by his mother and uncle. His mother supported the family through weaving.

As a young man, Dissanayake attended Southland Balika Vidyalaya and then went on to continue his education at St. Aloysius College. While Dissanayake was in school he contributed to magazines and often wrote articles for the Sinhala paper known by the name, *Ada.* It was not poetry that first drew Dissanayake to the arts; instead, he spent a great deal of time as a photographer, winning awards and competitions while he was in his twenties. The only writing he engaged in during his youth was a few efforts at short fiction. These works are now mostly lost.

After graduating from college he went on to become a teacher of science at Sacred Heart Convent, Galle. It was at this institution that he met his future wife, Indrani Pathirana. In the mid-80s the couple had two children and was living in Colombo. Dissanayake began work at the Head Office of the Cement Corporation and his wife found work at the Curriculum Development Center. They live in the city to this day.

It was in his forties that Dissanayake began to write seriously. He often wrote on topics of history and Buddhism. His first novel was published in 1998 and was titled, *Kat Bitha.* It was followed by *The Saadhu Testament* that same year. It was also in 1998 that Dissanayake won the State Literary Award for the Best English Novel. He was celebrated as the first Asian writer to be published in an electronic format.

In the early 2000s he wrote and published the works, *The Bastard Goddess,* in 2003, and *Thirst* in 2004. He has also published a collection of poems titled, *Inequality.* It was noted for its experimental style and interesting use of language. In 2007, he again won the State Literary Award for the Best English Novel. In 2013, he received the SAARC Literary Award distributed by the Foundation of SAARC Writers and Literature.

Daya Dissanayake is an award winning bi-lingual author, the only Sri Lanka to have won State Literary Award for English Novel thrice. He won it for the first time in 1998 for *Kat Bitha* which was his first novel. Eavesdropper won the award in 2007, and *Miracle under the Kumbuk Tree* in 2013. His *The Saadhu Testament*; is the first electronic novel by an Asian Author. He followed it up by releasing Wessan Novu Wedun also as an enovel thus becoming the first to publish a Sinhala Electronic Novel. Both books are available for free online reading at this website. He shared the Swarna Pusthaka Award for the Best Sinhala novel 2007 for 'Chadraratnage Bhavantara Charikava'.

Book Publications

Who was Ashoka? A Critical Study. 2019. Pakshighar, Bubhanneshwar.

Fiction

'Kat Bitha' – 1997. Author published. Sri Lanka. Historical novel based on Sigiriya.

Won the State Literary Award for the Best English Novel 1998.

'The Saadhu Testament' – 1998 www.saadhu.com – the First e-novel from Asia.

'The Healer & the Drug Pusher' 2000 – 1st print Universe. Vijitha Yapa, Colombo.

Historical novel based on the healthcare system in ancient Sri Lanka

'Inequality' – 2005. author published Poems

'Moonstone' – 2006. Sarasavi. Colombo – Contemporary Fiction

'Eavesdropper' 2006 – 1st print Ministry of Cultural Affairs. 2nd print Sarasavi. Colombo. Won the State Literary Award for the Best English Novel 2007

The Miracle Under the Kumbuk Tree – 2012 Sarasavi, Colombo Won the State Literary Award for the Best English Novel 2013

The Clone – 2012 – Serenity. A Historical Novel from the Future. Serenity, Colombo As e-books only

The Bastard Goddess – could the future Buddha be a woman?

Thirst – The Historical Environmentalist Novel

In Sinhala

'Vessan Novu Vedun' – 2003. Sinhala version of Healer & the Drug Pusher. First Sinhala E-novel

Chandraratnage Bhavanthara Charikava – 2006. Sinhala version of Moonstone. Shared the Swarna Pusthaka Award 2007.

Asa Sitiya Ohu Mese – 2008 – Sinhala version of *Eavesdropper*. Babli – 2010 – Sinhala version of Miracle under the Kumbuk Tree Kloniyakage Katha Vasthuwa – 2011 – Sinhala version of *The Clone* Pipasaya – Sinhala version of Thirst

Translations (from Sinhala to English)

Son of the Soil – 2010 Biography of a Deshamanya H. K. Dharmadasa (Nawaloka), written by Bandara Eheliyagoda.

Swayanjatha – 2011 – the Sinhala novel which won the Swarna Pusthaka Award 2008

Book Chapter

Mother is the Buddha at Home. The Concept of Motherhood in India. ed. Zinia Mitra. Cambridge Scholars Publishing. 2020.

Preface

This is my twentieth edited volume in the publication journey. I have faced many challenges though I wish to learn many from the previous experiences. Indeed, man learns from the past and this past is a reflection of present. The present is undoubtedly a reflection of future. I refer to this endless cycle of life because in my attempt to look into the writers of my neighbor countries, I find one in Daya Dissanayake whose writings have impressed me very much. This is my first critical volume on a foreign writer preferably from Sri Lanka. He is a novelist of many distinctions and merits. He focuses primarily on Ecology and Environment which attracted me as a reader. He has touched up on Ecological Wisdom in all his works. The literary works have won him the State Literary Award from the Government of Sri Lanka. His writings are recognised now. A few scholars are working for PhD theses which are but a good sign of development. Working on a writer from a foreign soil has given me an opportunity that put me in constant doubts whether I would be successful or not. The themes settings and locale are always challenging for the critics to get into the depths of native land, traditions and culture. This is how the job of a critic is to explore those elements from the foreign soil. The satisfaction puts me in a comfortable position today as I could collect a dozen papers on his novels. I wished to have a good number of papers but as God disposed, I should restrict them to a mere dozen. Time decides the destiny and I should believe in this concept since man works under circumstances either by choice or compulsion. Time has a way of showing us what really matters in life. Daya Dissanayake has been in India on several occasions in connection with seminars and conferences. He is a prolific writer and speaker too. His main concern is to protect environment and ecology. In fact, the world confronts them in every corner of the map. Deforestation, unusual climate changes, rapid rise in temperatures has ultimately put the world in peril. Social environmentalists have voiced their concerns just as literary environmentalists are doing them through priceless jewels of literature.

If one looks at the literary appreciation and critical appraisal in this volume, I think the critics have balanced between a routine study of thematic concerns and an application of literary theories and finally a good volume has come out before the readers. All the contributors of this volume have done a scholarly research on the novels of Daya Dissanayake. The volume begins with a jointly authored paper entitled "Life in the Limbo": A Reading of Daya Dissanayake's *Eavesdropper* --- SP Soubhaghya and Dr.NU Lekshmi. They have established that *Eavesdropper* satirizes the patriarchal society that has only contempt for women. As a major theme in the novel, the writer addresses the issues of women who are considered just as sexual objects. Patriarchy that holds dominance and is filled with detest towards women is portrayed through the character Tharanga, who considers women as reproductive machines. The second paper is contributed by Dr. Lily Arul Sharmila. She has evaluated the novel *The Healer and the Drug Pusher* for deeper realities. Daya Dissanayake's *The Healer and the Pusher*: A Manifestation of Deeper Reality is the title of paper. *The Healer and the Drug Pusher* is, according to Lily Sharmila, an epitome of the history and culture of the Indian people, the society of medieval Ceylon, ancient hospitals of Sri Lanka, ancient irrigation works of Ceylon, the annals of internal medicine, the asceticism and the art of healing in ancient India, the early history of Buddhism in Ceylon, and life and culture of ancient India. It is a rich legacy that the novelist has demonstrated through the representation of culture and tradition in South Asia. S. Malathy, an established critic, has dealt with "The Theme of Re-birth or Reincarnation: Astounding Revelation in *Moonstone*". According to her evaluation, "*Moonstone*", depicts the strange life of a protagonist who is prepared to commit\ a parricide to meet his ideal, his ultimate object of life. He is confident and constant in his attempt to make his father "be reborn", as his own biological son. To pursue his obsession he makes strenuous efforts, calculating the right time of conception and the right time his father should die. But the unexpected demise of his father deprives him of his chances of success. Another critic, Dr. Anita Arul has dealt with the theme of "Regression" from Daya Dissanayake's novel *Miracle under the Kumbak Tree*" for a critical evaluation. She concludes that the unintentional return to the past because of the shame and hurt is inevitable as it is a part of human condition. Facing unsolvable problems, desires not gratified during childhood daily make Babli get upset with things around. She often travels back carrying memorable events in order to get back to normal mood. Childish behavior of having doll with her "It is with her. She holds it to her chest when she goes to sleep. She keeps it with her on the table when she studies. She used to keep it in her school bag when she was a child" (90) and going back to past recalling some incidents can be a temporary relief for Babli. Later in her life time she became aware of some truth regarding life and started come out of brooding and tries to help her father in coming out of depression and starts treatment too. Babli too comes closer to nature and she is away from false memories too. Though the relationship between father Eddie and Babli is stubborn, "the bond, a paternal umbilical cord, would have been there always, invisible and dormant till today, till this moment" (99). In another brilliant paper, Dr. Anju S Nair has studied the novel *Moonstone* for inner journey in order to evoke consciousness. She sums up the novel as "*Moonstone* is an interesting and elusive novel. It is realistic and fantastic. All the incidents seem to take place in the physical and the mental world and this lends ambiguity to the novel. The novel is a complex work of idealism removed from the human conflict of conscience and love". It shows the awful consequences of a man's deliberate commitment to himself with a view to gratifying his pride and his ambition. We have another paper contributed jointly by Dr.Beula Hema latha and J.Miraclin. They have worked on the novel *The Healer and the Drug Pusher* for the study of Euthenics. It is entitled as "Capsulisation of Euthenics in Daya Dissanayake's *The Healer and The Drug Pusher*". Euthenics is a branch of science that aims to better different aspects of the environment in order to improve humans' wellbeing and/or the wellbeing of other living things. They explicated that the novelist explores the differences in lifestyle of people within a thousand years and shows that people nowadays blindly follow the advanced medication methods and food consumption. The author, throughout the novel, tends to inculcate his ideas to the younger generation about the harmful effects of drugs that people consume without hesitation. Renu Milind Dhotre, a research scholar from the University of Mumbai, has reviewed the novel *Miracle under the Kumbak Tree*. The review is by all standards a scholarly one as she has explored multiple themes from the novel. She sums up the review as "the book doesn't have an ending but a list of options that the protagonist could pursue further, leaving it to the reader's imagination. This also leaves scope for sequel of the book and there are many avenues for a spin-off" In yet scholarly paper by Dr. D. Vijayalakshmi, the central theme gets explored in terms of what Daya Dissanayake largely focused on. I can, without hesitation, put it as the best in terms of the Ecological Wisdom from his novels which move around the common theme. Her paper is entitled as "Exploring Ecological Wisdom in Daya Dissanayake's *The Clone*". According to her estimation, ecological wisdom is focused on with reference to Daya Dissanayake's *The Clone*. This study begins with a conceptual clarification so as to correctly define the focus and state the purpose of this research which is to read Daya Dissanayake's novel, *The Clone*, in the light of ecological wisdom. Secondly, principles of ecological wisdom and thirdly, scope and research perspectives on ecological wisdom are discussed. She further claims that there is a wider scope for further research in this area as there are a number of principles to be discussed under ecological wisdom by the great environmental writers. "The present research is limited to only two principles such as reverence to nature and holism. Furthermore, only one novel of Daya Dissanayake, who is a great lover of deep ecology, is taken into consideration out of his nine novels". We have another critic by name Dr. G. Sri Latha who is known for environmental concerns. She has studied the significance of title of the novel "A Critical Study on Significance of the Title *Thirst*". According to her scholarly evaluation, the novel 'Thirst' portrays the atrocious actions of the King. Throughout the novel the greediness of the King is evident. The King also exhibits pride and is adamant in each of his decisions. Due to such decisions the entire ecosystem is affected and disturbed. The novel opens with the Kings victory over conquering various territories. He immediately dreams of constructing a new palace. Then he goes ahead to construct a big dam. Every act of the King is associated with his self glorification. The title assumes greater significance in the light of ecological concerns. Dr. Palakurthy Dinakar, a veteran scholar, has studied "Filial Affection in Daya Dissanayake's *Miracle under the Kumbak Tree*". According to him, the novel *Miracle under the Kumbuk Tree* expresses the filial love of a daughter to her father. This is the story of Babli, a very methodical girl, the only daughter of Edward Silva and Jasintha Samaranayake, daily paid workers on the coconut estates around their remote village Mahakele about 5 km from Anamaduwa in Sri Lanka. Dr.S. Karthik Kumar has studied Daya Dissanayake's novel *Moonstone* for "Poverty of Wealth". According to Karthik Kumar, the novel is a brilliant example that depicts the hollowness of modern life. Life is meaningful only when it is lived. Life has to be experienced with its ups and downs and twists and turns. One cannot overpower the natural forces. One has to be ready to accept life as it comes. His research paper fulfills the standards of a quality paper when one looks at the amalgamation of poignant touches from English poetry. Any paper has to be innovative and analytical. Karthik has used poetry to justify the typical poetic touch and contextually applied it to this novel by Daya Dissanayake. One must remember the lines of Tennyson in "Tithonus"

> Why should a man desire in any way
> To vary from the kindly race of men
> Or pass beyond the goal of ordinance
> Where all should pause, as is most meet for all? ("Tithonus")

Sandaruwan may be a fictitious character. He justifiably concludes that Daya Dissanayake, through his character, represents the pitiable modern man who suffers from an inward void that cannot be filled by money and power but only by spiritual pursuit.

In the last paper, a scholarly one by Dr. R. Karthika Devi focuses on multiple dimensions like spiritual, psychological and philosophical and thrillers and pullers of suspense from the reading of novel *Moonstone* to a brilliant conclusion. Her paper is entitled "The Spiritual, Psychological, Philosophical, and Scientific Suspense Thriller-Elements in Daya Dissanayake's *Moonstone*" is really a gem of explorations by all standards. She concludes the novel with the Buddhist idea of the world as *maya* and refers to the eternally changing nature of the world. He has aptly given the last chapter the title 'Wheel' which symbolises the very nature of human life. Her evaluation of the novel brings out the many nuances of themes and other dimensions.

Thus, the novels of Daya Dissanayake, a Sri Lankan Writer, have been very meticulously evaluated in terms of significant themes as critics have explored in their papers. Towards the end, I hope that more research needs to be done on his novels. The little compass of this volume needs to be explored more in an extensive critical spectrum in future. In conclusion, I thank all the contributors for their painstaking efforts in bringing out this critical volume in a successful approach.

Dr. P.V. Laxmiprasad (Editor)
Karimnagar, Telangana

Contents

CHAPTER 1

Life in the Limbo: A Reading of Daya Dissanayake's *Eavesdropper*

S.P. Soubhaghya and N.U. Lekshmi

Daya Dissanayake, a bilingual Sri Lankan writer tries to demolish certain stereotypical beliefs of his native country. The rule of the colonial super powers incorporated various oppressive thoughts into the collective consciousness of the Sri Lankan people. Dissanayake who is thrice the winner of the State Literary Award, has to his credit various books that sow the seeds of optimism. His writings that endorse the harmony of human mind are free from aggression. His work *Chadraratnage Bhavantara Charikava* won the Swarna Pusthaka Award for the Best Sinhala novel in 2007 and *Kat Bitha* in 1998 received the State Literary Award for the Best English Novel. Though a bilingual writer, in an interview, Dissanayake says:

> In my column sometimes back (April 22, 2013) I commented that I am really ashamed to be bilingual, especially when I meet Indian writers and even businessmen, who are fluent in so many languages. In Sri Lanka I should have been bilingual in Sinhala and Tamil. Language is a man-made barrier which we have to overcome somehow. I use the colonial language to share my writing with those who cannot read our native language, but I have not become a slave to it, because I still have my feet firmly on the ground, and I can think in either language. And with most of my novels, I write simultaneously in both languages, which makes it very easy of me." (3)

The works of Dissanayake include *The Saadhu Testament, The Healer and the Drug Pusher, The Bastard Goddess*, *Thirst*, *Inequality*, *Moonstone* and *Eavesdropper*. *Eavesdropper* is a short novel written by Dissanayake which details the thought process of a lifeless man. The author at the beginning of the novel cites *Impossibility,* a work written by John D. Barrow to showcase "the Limits of Science and the Science of Limits" (3). Dissanayake by citing the work supports the idea put forth by Barrow which is quoted as Word processing

……… has altered the way in which writers think. Writers used to write because they had something to say; now they write in order to discover if they have something to say (3).

Eavesdropper is an extra-ordinarily surprising piece that affects the mind of the readers. The novel is narrated through the words of Tharanga, a man who lives with the help of machines. For the world around him, he is a comatose patient who is immobile. The protagonist of the novel can actually hear and feel things around him. He is put in a difficult situation where he is unable to find the real reason behind his immobility. He finds it hard to distinguish reality from dream. He says:

> I really don't know if i am on a bed in a hospital room, except from what I can hear. I don't know if am inside my body or outside. A soul, athma, gandabba, whatever, hovering above my body,dead/dying/undead/braindead. Then why am i unable to leave this room and roam free? Probably some connection to the body on the bed, a kind of umbilical cord, wire, magnetic force. Or i am imprisoned inside my own body, unable to leave it. Perhaps my soul got trapped inside, unable to leave my body with my last breath. Aladdin, please come and rub the lamp. I want to get out of my body. I will do anything you say. (10)

The introductory pages of the novel make the readers believe that the story is a dream process of the main character. A deep insight reveals that it is about a one man protest where the human mind is in a battle against the human body. While analysing the novel from a psychoanalytic perspective, it becomes clear that human mind is a powerful weapon that cannot be destroyed. Dreaming is in fact a process that requires detailed analysis and research. Researchers have proven that dreaming is a natural process similar to breathing, an activity that involves individual's participation without consent. According to various studies 20% of the total sleep time is devoted to dreaming. Psychological study of dreams that originated in the late 1800s considered dream as an escape mechanism. Reading through the pages of the novel makes the readers discover that Tharanga is not in a process of dream but is in an unknown state. He thinks that "Coma. Vegetarian State. Paralysis. I hear so many different names. If i am asleep I would not be able to hear anything. So i am not asleep….They would not know if i am seeing them or not. Like a dead man with eyes open" (81). The readers find it difficult to distinguish the real from the unreal.

Tharanga who is grown up in a rich family, is guaranteed with all the niceties of life. He enjoys a luxurious life with all its advancement. The novel can be seen as a critique of people who are addicted towards the superiority of money and power. Dissanayake is a writer who is against the dominance of money and power has effectively brought out the evils that persist in the name of wealth and authority. In an interview he clearly states that "Today there is no true freedom to write, to read, or to discuss what we read. All our creative work is monitored, censored or suppressed, either by those who hold power or wealth" (3).

Eavesdropper questions the overdominance of machines on human mind and body. Tharanga who lives at the mercy of the machines says:

> I have become the extension of the machines. Or the machines have become extensions of my body. It depends on the way we look at it. Do i control the machines or do the machines control me? What is more important, my body or the machines? If my mind could take over the machines i could outlive the machines, or the machines would take over my body and my mind. Anyway the machines will outlive me. They are made to work for years and years, save or kill as many patients as they can, and then get thrown into a junk yard or sold to another smaller hospital. (12-13)

Hospitals and machines are the power holders of today's society. For Tharanga if machines outlive him, his place will be replaced by another wealthy man. The bed-ridden Tharanga faces an internal conflict to find out the rationale behind his comatose state. The novel reveals the fact that the hidden truths of human lives are exposed only in secrecy. Due to this condition of Tharanga, he becomes aware of the truth that he is not the real inheritor of the family. Shalini, Tharanga's sister says to Ayesha "This bugger is not my brother. He is a bastard. I mean a real bastard. Born to some woman who never got married" (31). The words of Shalini pierce deep into the mind of Tharanga who is ready to accept the truth. He gives importance to relationships instead of acquiring money. The voice of the writer echoes in the character of the narrator. Tharanga is presented as a sharp contrast to his brothers. In a family that is business oriented, Tharanga's brothers can do anything according to their wish. This is evident in his words "The hospital can convert this room into an Intensive Care Unit, whenever they want. Anything is possible if one has the money and the right contacts. In hospital or in prison, money can provide all the luxuries, except freedom" (12). Tharanga considers his room as a stage where life is enacted as a play. His family members are unaware of the presence of Tharanga. They do not realise that Tharanga can hear everything that's happening around him. When everyone leaves the room to total silence Tharanga considers it as a state of intermission. It is at this point memory leaps into the mind of Tharanga. He says "Silence around me, in the night, leaves me only with my memories. Memories die only with the death of the brain. Till then we have to live with our memories. Pleasant and unpleasant" (82). At this juncture, Tharanga realises that memory is a bliss as well as a burden for him.

Eavesdropper satirises the patriarchal society that has only contempt for women. As a major theme in the novel, the writer addresses the issues of women who are considered just as sexual objects. Patriarchy that holds dominance and is filled with detest towards women is portrayed through the character Tharanga, who considers women as reproductive machines. Women are considered inferior and are good only to carry out domestic chores:

> Why don't they go home and get married and look after the husband and bring up children? That's what they are meant for. Anyway women should be put in their place. We should not let them start all this women's lib and such things....Women can never do anything right, except produce children, cook meals and wash clothes. See what has happened in every country which was governed by women? (78)

This attitude of Tharanga made him forsake his girlfriend Ivana. Ivana's love for him is genuine and is evident when she prays for the bed-ridden Taranga. The writer aptly titles the novel as *Eavesdropper* since its main character hears everything secretly even though it is not a deliberate act.

Another major concept used by the writer is dualism. The aspect of dualism that manifests itself in the mind of Tharanga, makes him compare purity and impurity, poor and rich, good and bad, man and animal, god and human and birth and death. Tharanga views death as the end of all sufferings whereas for him birth is just only a beginning of misery. The novel is written from a philosophical perspective and questions the universally accepted facts. His concept of death is revealed when he says "Then i would be dead. Death is total relaxation. Heaven. Moksha. Nirvana" (129). The world around Tharanga is filled with nothingness: "Nothing. What a fascinating topic. To me any way. Doing nothing, saying nothing, hearing nothing. There could be books written about nothing, poems, philosophical arguments. Religious discourses. Someone should do a film on nothing" (101).

Eavesdropper questions the social inequalities especially the clash between the rich and the poor. Tharanga compares rich people to poor people and the author opines that:

> Such high sounding diseases happen only to rich and the upper classes. Poor people don't get such things, because they often die before the illness is diagnosed. Either because they have only their hospital in the nearest town to treat them, or even if they are in the city, the government hospitals do not have the time and the facilities to diagnose and treat them, the waiting list for an MRI could be several months. Heart patients are waiting for a by-pass for several years. At least it proves that the patient could survive without the bypass. (84)

The lines authenticate that poor people have to be poorer and the rich will always get richer. *Eavesdropper* tries to deconstruct the socially accepted norms with the aid of various techniques like intersexuality, use of memory and blending the real with the unreal situations. On the whole, the novel is a reflection of human mind and the wickedness that society fosters.

Works Cited

Dissanayake, Daya. *Eavesdropper*. Sarasavi Publishers, 2006.

Barry, Peter. *Beginning Theory: An Introduction to Literary and Cultural Theory*. Manchester UP, 2009.

Barnes, Hazel, E., translator. *Being and Nothingness*. By Jean-Paul Sartre, Washington Square, 1956.

Linn, Denise. *The Hidden Power of Dreams: How to Use Dream on Your Spiritual Journey*. 2nd ed., Hay House, 2009

CHAPTER 2

Daya Dissanayake's *The Healer and the Drug Pusher* – A Manifestation of Deeper Social Reality

Lily Arul Sharmila

A novel belongs to the sphere of literature called fiction. It is meant to be read. It has plot character, dialogue and the atmosphere. The novel as long as the writer wants it to be not to suffer from the great economy in the handling of plot, characters and dialogue and superficial materials. The novelist conforms to several material requirements. The fictionist takes liberties to preach or make propaganda that smooth is just product meant only to increase the profit of MNC's Dr. Ravi said '*Money he earned was good, much more than most of his friends in other jobs*'. (P 31) The author takes a comprehensive view of the whole civilisation. The novel aims at revealing the meanings, principles and social styles that govern people's lives. The actions of the individual are scrutinised in the light of the civilisation that surrounds them. The novel explores the modern society dominated by the corrupt business class. The characters are viewed as a part of a developing environment, the splendor and shame of modern civilisation. The writer sketches the different stages in the growth of his consciousness. A great novel is formed on the structure of a contrast, concerning moral themes and expressing human feelings and motives through characters from the different worlds of 10th century and 20th century.

Those days the doctor would explain what was wrong; tell us how it could have happened and the treatment they were giving. Now we don't know anything and just have to come and watch her lying on the hospital bed. Don't you think that we have a right to know? The doctors are too busy; they will not have any time to treat the patients. (45)

The novel deals with human foibles, fallacies, infidelities and desires. Subject captures varied layers of human existence. The texture locates in its socio-cultural context. The imaginative product examines a range of themes borders on ancient andmodern world. It is a concern of the writer for the realm of humanities thus indicating the need for a broader consensus and a view of society and history. The chapters provide a detailed analysis of commodity derivatives growing in popularity as an investment tool. The derivatives are a financial investment whose value is derived from the assets. The story critically examines the demarcation between commodity and human security. The fiction encompasses a range of subjects. It brings independent ideas and some fresh insights raising a set of highly pertinent question with regard to comprehending the complex issues like structures of administration and policy that accompany the aspirations of the man and commitment to the quantifiable collectives. The more rigidly constructed categories created by institution, corporate organisation are brought to the focus. The issues enlarged upon here are the living stratum of the people in the 10th century and in 20th century the novel remains a relevant and pertinent concept of the economy that clocks the growth. The novelist puts in perspective his credibility and convictions on the ultra-conservative kingdom. These narratives as discursive endeavors are certainly commendable in its broad scope and the depth of human potential. Main characters in the 10th century are as follows.

In the 10th century

Minda – a fisherman in small Tamil village in Jaffna, somewhere near thepresent Vallipuram

Kita – Minda's son

Sankar – a Tamil Buddhist village 'headman' and official at the hospital

Basu – Sankar's son

Pali – Sankar's daughter

Mitra – Persian sailor of the Christian faith

Channa – Buddhist physician priest at hospital in Jaffna

Stiya – a Sinhala girl from the south of Sri Lanka

Namibia – Another Sinhala girl

In the 20th century

Thangaraja – a Tamil Tea Factory officer in the country

Raju – Thangaraja's son

Chitra – Raju's wife

Bhanu – Their Daughter

Sumanadasa – a Sinhala friend of Raju

Kumari – Sumanadasa's wife

Suneeta – Their daughter

Gunadasa – Sumanadasa's brother

We anticipate Daya in his social criticism and satire during this new era of artistic refinement, thematic liberalism and stylistic innovations in order to reach artistic perfection. His novel deals with respectable country, society and presents aminiature world dominated by both conservative and materialist realms. Like a historical novel he combines picturesque details with sentimental feelings for the past. He makes use of elements of records and soul suffering to heighten a human story of values introducing greater human interest and pathos. He is supreme in depicting the life using his novel as a platform for social reform. He moralises and his weapons for social criticism and reform are irony and satire. The novel contains philosophical observations on religion, politics and morals. Daya has taken characters from 10th century personages and portrayed the innermost soul of his characters with great insight, affection and values. The well managed discourses impart vividness and actuality to the story and the personages. The dialogue reveals the passions and emotions of characters advanced by the movement of the plot. The speeches of the characters are natural, appropriate and dramatic keeping with the personality by the speaker. The novel studies the relationship between the ancient systems of philosophy and medicine. It explores the mutually dependent relation between the mind and the body (Chinese system). The novel demonstrates as the ancient medical traditions can be used for improvingthe physical and mental health of people today. The book unravels the anatomy of a historic step towards perfect equilibrium between past and present.

The central concern of the novel lies in conceptualising a contemporary andmaterialistic attitude of the people. It examines the diversity of the images and practices from the consumerist spectacle. In the chapter titled 'The side effects of the drugs' Raju defends the doctors. Mehamedna examined him 'those days the doctor would explain what was wrong, tell us how it could have happened and the treatment they were giving. Now we do not know anything and just have to come and watch her lying on the hospital bed. We do not know how serious her condition is. Don't you think that we have a right to know? The great skill and insight in thenovelist demanded by the characterisation lie in the art of presenting the charactersalive and real to our imagination. The men and women in the story move through like living beings in the memory of readers. The writer creates the characters from outside, directs their passions, thoughts and feelings. The characters are allowed to reveal themselves through speech and action and the comments of other characters.

Raju had to stop every few steps to talk to either a fellow marketing person or the hospital employee or a doctor and he wondered why his daughter could not realise that he knew all these people because of his profession and how useful contacts were (44)

The story provides the significant perspectives that Raju markets pharmaceuticals and he ignores his daughter Bhanu's rebellious attitudes towards him. According to her the drugs kill more people than tobacco and alcohol. The big drug companies manufacture drugs making profit. The drugs are as harmful as illegal drugs. Raju could not understand his daughter's attitude. Bhanu, the well-disciplined girl with traditional and cultural values hails from Tamil Hindu family. Chitra and Raja came to know of Suneetha's liver damage and a liver transplant. Suneetha is victimised by the possible adverse effects of drugs. The multi-national companies use people in our country as their guinea pigs. Now they think of going to Anuradhapura where a Buddhist priest who knows some good physicians. They leave for Anuradhapura. People in these villages still show the typical Lancan hospitals. They don't offer a meal showing off their wealth or expecting some favour in return. A curry is made of sesame seeds a variety of ash pumpkin, green leaf salad, a different varieties of leaves plucked from the garden Asheaf of betel is offered. 'Don't worry about anything. She doesn't need any surgery. You don't have to take her anywhere. There is a very simple remedy for this condition.' Siyatu paused. Palli, Sankar's daughter and Mitra the Persian Sailor of Christian faith are introduced to each other through the subject of conversation that borders on the vegetation that is raised by Sankar's diligent labour. Palli's world opens up to the natural phenomenon and its bounty which brings her close to Mitra who is patronised by the officials of the hospital. A huge space is unfolded by the novelist reiterating upon the need for communion with the world of nature that abounds in the pictures farming in the village harvesting vegetables and rearing goats. The representatives are Palli, Basu children of the village head man Sankar. The Wounded Mitra once blind can see. Badaakara Hospital is almost like his home. Hecan see the world around him. He can plan for his future. He tells Palli 'I want to learn medicine. I want to learn all I can about treating eye ailments, so that I canhelp other people like me who have gone blind. So I want to say as many people from this fate as I can' (123).

The novel of Daya portrays life on a broader level dealing with a slice of life of people in the 10th century and 20th century. This novel as a literary composition is an off shoot of the interest of the writer in other men. The novelist presents the great panorama of human passion and action. The compounded of thesome stuff gets bound up with literary elements. It is like a pocket theatre, a long narrative in prose detailing the actions of the imaginary people. The first chapter titled "The Cast Away" details the livelihood of the fisherman Minda. The episodedraws out generally the simple life of Minda, his son Kita in a rambling manner.

'*The Healer*' is a loose form of art that helps the writer to present a complete and more varied representation of real life with the summation of actual living. The story combines within itself the narratives, descriptive passages, historical frame work philosophical speculations, imaginative vigour, social critique and specifically the ideas of life. The novel deals with the events and actions and the manner in which these are depicted are immensely appreciable. The men and women are involved in these events are the characters in the novel interacting among themselvesthrough the element of dialogue.

As healing became a part of Buddhism, all the medical knowledge needed tobe collected in early monasteries so it came institutionalised, attached to monasteries and grew into hospitals. Brahmins incorporated the medical practices with rituals and Vedic practices. To improve the efficiency of the healing plants they created a plant goddess Arundati and a God Kushta. Mitra is helped by the team of doctors in the monasteries hospital and the Buddhist headman of the village.

Medicine has been very close to Buddhism. There are some teachers who believe that four noble truths where based on the medical theory of suffering, its cause, its suppressions and the method of its elimination which seems so similar. (23)

Being away from frantic rush, mind finds much needed rest and people do not glimpse into the chaos of the city but spend the days in their personal garden, a dip in the infinity and have a rejuvenating moment. A sea gull, dark blue sea, cloud, palmyah trees, coast line, glittering water stimulate the curing process.

Minda a fisherman in small Tamil village in Jaffna near Vallipuram supplied fish to the hospital, a pave of monastery where there was a statue of Buddha. Mindacould see the Buddha's face from the boat. He believed that those gentle kind eyesof Buddha would be fixed on them and could protection them from any danger they might encounter. Kita, Minda's son would inherit the profession when his father becomes too old to go on the boat. After supplying the quantity of fish required bythe hospital, any extra fish left over would be taken to the market. The least valued smaller fish would be taken home for dinner. It was their only income. They did not have any other land for farming.

The novel indicates the flow of outer experiences of the flux of thoughts in men. The novelist records the random but logical flow of impressions passing through the characters to stamp the mental activity of the persons in all minute details. It shows the minds of the characters in such a manner as to reflect the unending activities of the mind with all apparent irrelevances and contradictions. The novelist generally employs the conventional syntax to symbolise the chaotic nature of the human consciousness. The story gives the picture of the lives of the characters through the delineation of their actions and thoughts representing the influences of the region and locality on a group of characters. In the first chapter of these novel local peculiarities are given prominence with the description of the traits in a realistic manner. A kind of uniqueness is archived through thematic variations and fascinating depictions of two different phenomena.

Sankar said, "there had been a boy named Kashyapa who lived in India about 1500 years ago. He was the son of a philosopher named Ulka. Once on a Pilgrimage with his father he had noticed that thousands of Pilgrims who were coming to the river Ganges were scattering flowers and rice on the road. While all the other were praying and bathing in the river, this boy started collecting the scattered grains of rice. A sage who was passing bystopped and asked the boy why he was collected the discarded rice grains whicheven the beggar would not care to collect. A single grain of rice is as important as all the riches in the world". (52)

The objective of the novel is to take a central figure through a succession of scenes and adventures and to introduce a great number of characters around and thus builds up a picture of society. It acquaints the readers with the social life and the presentation of several human situations. The dynamic movements of the characters construct the complex relationship between good and evil. The characters reveal strange truth that generous impulses exist even them whom society considers to be conflicting phenomena.

The whole setting of the story is set on both social and material, the sea life, the life of different classes of people with regional background. The scope of the novel has been widened by means of including almost all the modern subjects. Through this medium of novel the author reaches the public to reiterate the fact that some special herbs or materials needed for the preparation of medicines to bring cure upon the man wounded and his boat reached the shore with the help of the fishermen. The Stranger Mitra must be from a faraway country Persia sailing in a tradingvessel. Mitra has been working in trading vessels for many years. Now Mitra is ina hospital, a part of the Buddhist monastery at Badakara, in Sri Lanka. The Junior Physician Mahamedna explained that the immersion theraphy was for the treatmentof his son burst skin and to bring down his fever. In some cases, essence of meat has to be used in the preparation. Immersion theraphy and medicine were developed and practiced by the Buddhist monks long before Hindus adopted them.

The story attempts to convey the spirit, manners and social condition of the past age with realistic details and nearly perfect fidelity to historical facts. The subject matter encompasses both public and private events with the detailed picture of the varied features of life of a particular age. The most important feature of the novel is its vivid reproduction of the life of the bygone age. As a result of the impulse towards novelty, there is a combination of social and economic changes which create proper climate for the emergence of the content of the novel. The Memory and imagination serve the creative purpose and the central narrative is constituted by thestrong life of humanity.

Those people who are considered to be of lower casts. These early physicians were mostly wonderingascetics. They treated people wherever they went, and also met and exchanged their knowledge and experience, getting into discussions and debates and thus went on accumulating all the medical lore into a huge store of medical information. (23)

Health is the condition of being sound in body, mind or spirit. It is a state of complete physical, mental and social well-being not merely the absence of disease or infirmity The story *The Healer and the Drug Pusher* goes back to a thousand years, to the last century before He dawn of this millennium, when perhaps people lived a healthier life. The plot of novel by Daya is a work of fiction, historical and modern and based on archaeological research carried out in Sri Lanka. All the characters and incidents in the book have no existence and have no relation to any person.

The novel allots a prominent position to the actual historical figure because the chief object of the novelist is the interpretation human character. He presents faithfully the manners, tone and temper of the age to bring creative imagination to bear upon the dry facts of history and to produce a work of artistic splendor. The fictional narrative focuses on the varieties of human behavior in society and the way in which the characters reflect or contradict the values of the society. Here the characters are seen in the background of their social milieu and culture. Though the inner life of the characters finds a place in the novel, the greater importance is accorded to their conflicts and collisions with classes and beliefs. Based on the different concepts of values, the essence of a novel lies in the conflict between the individual and society.

The organisation of matters in the novel relates the theme of substantial value and human interest. The plot is primarily concerned with the things which make life difficult, strenuous, intense and morally significant. The way in which these elements are organised achieves a definite artistic purpose. There is a gallery of characters in *The Healer and the Drug Pusher.* The characters belong to the 10th century are Minda, a fisherman in a small village in Jaffna. Kita was his son. Sankar was a Tamil Buddhist vitage headman and official at the hospital. Sankar's son was Basu. Pali was his daughter. The Persian Sailor of the Christian faith injured and was later saved by the fisherman Minda and his son Kita. Channa was a Buddhist physician priest at hospital in Jaffna.

The novelist has portrayed the characters from the world of Twentieth century too (Thangaraja, a Tamil tea factory officer in the hill country, Raju Thangaraj's son, Chirtra Raju's wife, Bhanu their daughter, Sumanadasa, Sinhala friend of Raju, Humain Sumandala's wife suneeta their daughter, Gunadasa Sunanadas's brother. The characters in the novel are many and multi-dimensional and they evolve with huge scope. The characters undergo sufferings to preserve their morality and integrity. (Mitra, Pali, Bhanu and Suneetha) The characters struggle hard to keep virtues against repeated attempts to outrage their honor. Daya's skilful organisation of several traits and qualities is beyond measures. He details human figures with their own motives and capacity for distinctive speeches and actions.

The sketches loosely woven together soon evoke satiric reactions. The characters at the centre move on the circumference of the story. The Tea factory officer wanted to see his son become a doctor Thangappa son Raju markets pharmaceuticals He works in a pharmaceutical company. They import and sell medicine. The post is called the medical representative. They promote the medical products but one can see the contrast in the outlook of father and daughter, Raji and Bhanu. Bhanu, Well disciplined, behaved friendly and respectful girl, brought up by his parents who taught her the traditional and cultural values of Tamil Hindu girl educated in Colombo.

Aiming at the inwardness of experience, the author effaces himself and the narrative progresses on the memory of the characters. The novel documents the world of the sense and describes the sensations and feelings of the characters. There are lengthy dialogues and number of correspondents including didactic strain with the manual of manners and decorum. The characters are part of the machinery of the plot. The qualities of character determine the action which changes the characters. There is an intense action which is the main attribute of a dramatic novel.The novel provides a realistic speculation about possible future events based solidlyon the adequate knowledge of the real world of past and present and on the thorough understanding of the human nature.

The other characters of the modern 20th century world are delineated as the imaginative creations, personages – a Tamil Tea factory officer in the hill countryand his family members his son Raju his wife Chitra, their daughter Bhanu, a Sinhala friend of Raju Sumanddasa their daughter and brother Suneeta and Gunadasa. The whole story has been read by Bhanu in the e-book when she is surfing the web forAncient medical care. She wanted to tell someone about the story of a blind traderand the wonderful medical facilities available in Sri Lanka over a thousand year ago.She tries to picture life of Pali. The separatist struggle, politician's problem, ethnicreligious conflicts never end. Bhanu had a series of mental images of Jaffna. Shevisualises the life of Pali. She hears of Keerimalai, Mavittapuram Temple, and the ruins of Buddhist temples. She decides to tell Sumanadasa about what she read to persudehim to arrange a visit to the place.

The people of our present times hence lost their faith in the medicines produced art of herbs. The herbs or any oils needed for the treatment cannot be found. People cannot find any pure beels honey. But in those days are person would ran home for mee oil another for honey and to collect the plants they run into the jungle and the women there to pound it and prepare the necessary medication. The cancer drugs they make now in modern times bring big money. It is a multibillion dollar business. They keep manufacturing and the doctors keep on prescribing till anyway the patient dies in the end. The manufacturer and the doctor know that it will not cure the cancer but they both fill their pockets.

The novel offers a nuanced critique of historical and modern and is based onarchaeological research carried out in Sri Lanka. All the characters and incidents inthe book are imaginary and have no relation people what so ever to any person. Thisstory goes back a thousand years to the last century before the dawn of this millennium when perhaps people lived a healthier life. Most people who talked about the Y2K had forgotten or were not aware of HFA/2000. The WHO Slogan – Health For all by year 2000 which we have not been able to archive. 'May all living creatures be healthy' is the motto of Daya. He enriches his fiction with a long series of pictures that revolve around the phenomena of ancient hospitals of Sri Lanka. Ancient irrigation works of Ceylon, annals of internal medicine, asceticism and the art of healing in ancient India, early history of Buddhism in Ceylon, early settlements in northern Sri Lanka, education in Sri Lanka, food and the people historiography in a Time of ethnic conflicts. India in Ceylonese history, society and culture life and culture in ancient India, society medieval celyon and the history of culture of the Indian people. Day's work expresses the world outside him, mingling with the action and passion and feeling and thoughts of the people. He touches all aspects of experience characterised by charm, propriety and harmony. He holds upon the readers, imagination and intensifies their enjoyment.

Daya's fiction *The Healer and the Drug Pusher* is an epitome of the history and culture of the Indian people, the society of medieval Ceylon, ancient hospitals of Sri Lanka, ancient irrigation works of Ceylon, the annals of internal medicine, the asceticism and the art of healing in ancient India, the early history of Buddhism in Ceylon, and life and culture of ancient India

Works Cited

Dissanayake, Daya *The Healer and the Drug Pusher*, ISBN 955-96508-2-3, 2000

Majumdar, RC. *The History and Culture of the Indian people. 1954.*

Gunawardena. *Historiography in a Time of Ethnic conflict*, 1995

Life and Culture in Ancient India. B.N. Luniya 1978

Social History of Early Ceylon. H. Ella walla 1969.

CHAPTER 3

The Theme of Re-Birth or Re-Incarnation: An Astounding Revelation of Moonstone

S. Malathy

Sri Lanka, an island country, in the Northern Indian Ocean has been known under various names overtime. Being the biggest island in the South Asian context, Lanka has probably become an exclusive term for it. It was called 'Serendivis' by the Romans, 'Serandib' by the Arabs and 'Serendip by the Persians while the Greeks termed it 'Sielen Diva' or Siel diba. From the word 'Sielen', the British rulers derived the English form 'Ceylon' (1815-1972) Helabime meaning 'Land of Healas', is a name that Sinhalese were called by. The name is glassed as 'abode of lions' and attributed to a supposed former abundance of lions on the island. The name Sri Lanka was introduced by the Marxist Party (1935) in the context of Independence Movement for the British Ceylon. It was called 'The Republic of Sri Lanka', and later 'Democratic Socialist Republic of Sri Lanka', by the constitution of 1972 and 1978, respectively (en.m.wikipedia.org).

Sri Lanka marks a higher rate of literacy with its innate traditional sense and imbibed art of narrating long stories. The power impetus that Buddhism has and had on scholarships and literature excels in its writings. Ingenious works in prose and verse of the country which have drawn heavily from Buddhist parables are commendable. Their progressive aptitude for contriving has enabled them to analyse and discuss elaborately and clearly on the most challenging, complex aspects of philosophy, its concepts and ideas. These ideological precepts are admonished through stories taken from the life of Buddha and Jathaka stories (narratives of the past lives of Siddhartha Gauthama.

The ethnic conflict between the Sri Lankan Government and The Liberation Tigers of Tamil Eelam and its brief, but bloody conflict with Janata Vimukthi Peramuna which had lasted for 26 years caused a great disaster that involved violence. The theme of violence has become a significant one in the contemporary Sri Lankan Literature, during the period of war and its aftermath. Novelists like Gunasekaran, Medawattegedra and others have started focusing on several discrete sections of people, their experiences, memories and guilt. (www.researchgate.net) Whereas the writings of Daya Dissanayake, often features the subjects of non-violence, history, archaeology, Buddhism and how people perceive and adopt religion in their lives. From the land of Sri Lanka which has witnessed a turbulent, tumultuous, long ethnic strife, comes a saner voice, which reverberated the resonance of literature with its fathomless voice. Daya Dissanayake is an award winning, bi-lingual novelist, poet and blogger. He has paid unremitting attention to evoke peace among the people. Through his persistent application he has promoted a greater scope for humanity. Like a monk, he has deliberately eschewed violence, sex and hatred, because his main intention is to promulgate a better world of love. His writings enhance and ensure hope to the humanity. It illumines a sense of inner harmony and inculcates peace in the minds of people.

Daya Dissanayake, as Regi Siriwardena upon examination of "Miracle Under the Kumbuk Tree", denotes: "gives us an evocative portrayal of a world we see daily, but do not perceive – the rural underclass – a culture incredibly foreign to snug Colombian gatherings – perhaps dangerously so"... (en.m.wikipedia.org). Being a reformer of sorts, he hangs his thoughts, on seething issues. His greatest virtue is that he sees Sri Lanka steadily as a whole. He strenuously strives to propagate peace and harmony through his writing. While answering Jaydeep Sarangi, he states, "I believe that writing can change a society. At present most popular writing is thriving on violence and the dark side of humanity. We should strive for writings that highlight peace and harmony and love, not only for the humanity, but all the life on earth...."

Dissanayake, in his youth had contributed to the school magazines. He has written articles for the Sinhala paper 'Ade'. He is the only Sri Lankan writer to receive the Sri Lanka State Literary Award for the best English novel, three times. He has been awarded SAARC Literary Award (2013) for his first novel, Katbitha (1998) which has also won the State Literary Award (1998) The Healer and the Drug Pusher (2000) has comeout as the first POD book from Sri Lanka and its Sinhala version "Vessan Novu Vedun" (2003) became the first e-book in Sinhala. His novel "The Saddhu Testament" (1998) is the first e-novel in Asia. He is regarded by many to be the first Sri Lankan advocate for electronic books and self-publishing. His "Chandraratnage Bhavanthara Charikava" (2006) has been short-listed for the first ever Swarna Pusthaka Award (2007). The two versions of his new novel "*Moonstone*" (2006) in English and Sinhala have been published simultaneously. Though bi-lingual writers are scarce in all countries, Dissanayake excels in his art of writing. His bi-lingual versions remain unique and they are free of any adaption or transcreation, as he can think and create in both languages, effortlessly. They are genuine co-creations, yet independent of each other; they mark a distinct event not only in Sri Lanka, but elsewhere. For example Samuel Beckett a bi-lingual as well, has published his two versions in English and French, but not simultaneously.

Dissanayake's novel in English, titled '*Moonstone*' reflects on his mastery over the Sinhala language. The three names, taken by his protagonist to suit the three roles he adopts outline the depth of his knowledge in Sinhala. The protagonist takes the name Chandraratne, meaning 'moon gem' in Sinhala, in his first life or role, during his stay in Sri Lanka; he calls himself Sandaruwan – 'hela', more euphonious version of Chandraratne, in his second life or role on his stay in America; thirdly, he chooses another name called Chandare – a Common name, yet meaning moon, on his return to Sri Lanka. These names link his three states of life in sequence and it stands for the one and the same man who is following three different life styles / phrases.

Dissanayake is a creative genius. He is trendy and alert in his style. He has a keen eye for observing details. In "Moonstone", the novelist has skillfully woven the new information technology into the texture of the novel. His hero, Sandaruwan, an IT businessman who has settled in an island off La Digne Seychelles, is running Thakshana.com. He is a billionaire businessman rivaling Bill Gates. Being an IT typhoon, he is able to operate his entire global business empire from his house, "Supaditi" which is a true example of a global village. All the vegetables that Sandaruwan likes to eat are cultivated on the island home with uninterrupted power and water supply. Sandaruwan's residence and office are self-sufficient. With no secretary or office assistant as such, his offices are scattered around the world. He has real potential and knowledge and carries out his job, effectively. His efficacy has seldom failed / checked. With a skeleton staff, in perfect adequacy he has modified his room "which was for Sandaruwan's use only" (14) and "where (often) he spends the entire day and night" (13) He considers his equipment as an extension of himself to convert his thoughts into action via keyboards or microphone. He receives responses via the display, the printers or speakers. "His chair itself is more like a comfortable bed, where he could sit in any position he wished. His keyboard like everything else in the room is cordless." (13) The most wonderful thing, is his body clock which has started to adjust gradually as per his needs and whims. During his early days of building his empire, as he had to travel frequently or when he has to meet / work with clients from all over the globe, this kind of adaptability is of much help that served his purpose. Even after flying for hours and hours, he gets fully recharged with a few minutes of sleep on his working chair.

Sandaruwan has got only limited friends / visiting business associates over the globe. He doesn't believe in holding regular parties or dinners. Occasionally he invites a few to his island. But they have always been accommodated in a resort hotel in a nearby island. On seeing his house they exclaim: "This is what paradise would be like" (16). But they seldom know anything about his obsession. His obsession about his father, Romiel, or his troubled inner psyche that struggles: "He had one worry nagging at his mind all the time. His father was his problem. The only problem which could not yet be solved with all his knowledge, power and money" (22) When Sandaruwan gets his green card, he decides to leave Chandraratne (his first name-role) behind, in Sri Lanka, (where he has started his life from – his place of birth) dead and buried and forgotten. He prefers his stay in America because he believes that it is the only country where he can learn and do what he wants and where he can live his life the way he likes. Hence he chooses a new name, for his second role/life and allows his first role to go unnoticed, dead and buried. Whenever he gets a blurred image of his father that appears on one of his monitors, as a reflection, covering whatever is on display, he finds it difficult to concentrate on his work. One can never repay one's mother and father who have brought him up, fed and guided through his life. As he is brooding over: "Success and wealth never brought happiness or peace of mind", is indelible.

When he sits down at his elaborate dining table at Seychelles, he recollects the chipped enamel plate and how his father had been serving, "plain red rice with curry of ash plantains, pumpkin, golden melon or snake gourd, fresh green leaves and often there was some kinds of dried fish" (31) Whereas his father has always been managing with a loaf of bread or a few roties for the whole day whenever he (Chandraratne) is not around. Sandaruwan who loses all his desire to eat laments on his lost (last) life, which he cannot forbid, as he is trapped now, in his present life. Unable to promulgate a comfortable life to his father, he regrets on his condition. Being addicted and adopted to his wealthy life, he is destined to adept to eat, dress and live like every other billionaire in the society. It is highly improbable and impossible for Sandaruwan to live or imitate Romiel, who has no desire for any materialistic thing. Hence he nurtures a strange notion. As he is so obsessed with his father, and to live with his father he wants to improvise a dream, a belief: he yearns his father to be reborn as his own son. He who is so desirous, affirms that he can look after and "provide all sorts of comforts and luxuries and payback with interest what his father had done for him" (41)

On reading an article on rebirth, he is left to choose between a natural rebirth from a fertilised ovum or cloning. His first option is to clone his son using his father's DNA. He starts to probe: If he clones a child, how can he merge his father's mind-state into the child? To achieve this, his father has to die anyway at the correct time. His second option is to have a child from his own cells. For this he has to fertilise his sperm with the egg from a woman and the resultant embryo has to be implanted in a surrogate mother. Then, he realises that, the child he gets may only be a replica of Sandaruwan and so, he drops that idea. Even if he somehow manages to get a few cells from his father's body, the child he gets may only be like his father, and not his father. The clone may be a sort of younger twin and it may not be an exact replica except in appearance. It will only be a 'duplicate' and not an 'original'. Romiel's clone will be like Romiel's brother. If the clone is produced from Sandaruwan's DNA, then its parents will be Romiel and Swarnalatha, and it will be, physically Sandaruwan's brother and not his son, though legally Sandaruwan can claim the child to be his son. He gives up the idea of cloning because "A human clone is a total confusion in society, in law and in astrology"

(53) and a clone can never be his father. His only option is to have his own biological son not immediately, but at an exact time so that he can merge Romiel's mind-state continuing in the child.

To execute his ideal plan, he starts to search for his father's horoscope. He checks a little book that has been in his possession ever since the day of his mother's death. Swarnalatha, his mother, has entered into that the date and time of birth of Romiel, Chandraratne and Swarnalatha. Often, Sandaruwan, who gets haunted: "Why did mother have to die so early in his life? (35) and recollects the day on which she happens to die while picking chillies from their land. Before swooning to death, she starts to scream aloud saying "something bit her" (66). She has been bitten by a snake, she faces her untimely death. Sandaruwan believes that she must have known her life is short and that's the reason why 'she has stayed close to the temple and remained a devout Buddhist.

Sandaruwan who has started working on his now project, which he calls "project Omri' (6) imagines his father's reaction when he arrives home and states: "his father could take him for a ghost, not a thief (7). To him" "Home was only the house where his father lived. That was all. It was not home for him. Not since the day his mother had died. He had no idea how the house would appear after so many years, or if the house would be there at all" (6). He wishes his 'mission of mercy', a success: "his intentions were good and gods would look after him and help him to achieve his goal". (7) He enthusiastically starts his trip from Seychelles to Sri Lanka. On his way home, he identifies a landmark, a temple which he used to see often on his way to Colombo from home, so many years ago. He feels glad to realise that the "gods were still with him' (8) as he is able to identify things – a good omen.

Sandaruwan gets disturbed with an assemblage of questions: "Was he thinking of Chandraratne? Was he expecting his son to come home to see him? Did he know that Chandraratne was dead and Sandarawan was now settled down in the Seychelles?" (29) His memory lane goes back into his past life, first life (role). From the day he has entered the school in the town he has started to adjust himself into a life style of what has been universally accepted as the civilised world. The civilised world he has entered had alienated him from nature and from fellow human beings". (77) The gap widened day by day. Chandraratne like many other students at the Colombo University seldom speak about his home, parents or where he is coming from. Though he has no bitter reasons such as a broken family, a father who is drunkard, a quarrelsome mother or no family etc., he doesn't want to go home. Even after establishing his vast empire, he gives up his plan of visiting his father. Or, taking Romiel from the village in Sri Lanka to Seychelles. He believes that it can never work out as there is nothing original in such thoughts and it will ever remain a far-fetched story. To elucidate, he tells a story of Tolstoy in which the Russian ladies who cry at the theatre, stay oblivious to their coachmen, who are waiting outside in the freezing cold. He who has got used to much greater comforts, starts to enjoy more and more benefits of the advancing civilisation. He imbibes an idea that he is born again after reaching Los Angeles, by changing his name from Chandraratne to Sandaruwan, and begins to enjoy his new life. As he concludes: "Chandraratne was dead for all practical purposes. He had a new life now. A rebirth or a re-incarnation" (30).

Sandaruwan, who prefers to live alone, decides to obtain the ovum from a woman, without marrying her. Then he prepares the horoscope of the woman of his choice and publishes the same. Finally he selects Malrenu from Sri Lanka. After several correspondences, she comes to Sweden with her mother. They are offered a comfortable stay, gifted a traveler's cheque for 20,000 dollars, allowed to buy whatever they want to and are assured to be free of their excess baggage on the flight back. Having a great time, experiencing a boundless joy for the first time in their lives, they started to enjoy their trip. Malrenu who is been waiting to express her gratitude, is asked to meet the doctor, on a day, for a routine medical checkup, to see whether they are biologically compatible. The doctor who has successfully collected the egg from Malrenu, is been instructed to fertilize it with Sandarewan's sperm not immediately, but at an exact date and time. The doctor goes by the verbatim of his rich client, is not curious about any other details.

When Sandaruwan goes to his village on the fixed date and time, to his utter dismay he finds his father lying dead on the bed. He gives an injection to the day, Romiel's only companion and then places the dead dog close to his father. By emptying a bottle of petrol and dropping the bottle lamp on the bed, he sets the funeral pyre at 03.44. He gets puzzled to realize how he has been pursuing a mirage, all these days; how his total obsession has turned out to be meaningless, and how it has got shattered, so suddenly. He gets so frustrated. Without the exact time of death, there is no possibility of tracing out Romiel's place of birth in his next life. Lifting-off his great burden, for he has narrowly escaped from the act of parricide, he heaves a sigh of relief. Yet his relief is short-lived. As his thought goes back, he shamefully acknowledges his guilt that "he would have killed him, with the same drug which he had injected into the dog" (79) A patricide is in thought, though not in action. Unable to conceal, he feels that the time has come to end his life, his second role, even.

The one and the only reason for Sandaruwan to wish for a child is to have his own father as his son. But Romiel's unexpected death marks an abrupt end to his dream. Now that has gone beyond reach, he ponders: why should he go on making money? The question that disturbs him made him think deeply. Hence, he severs all his connections with Thakshana.com. He shuts down his computer and switches off his phone, erasing all the data on the chips and the phone memory. Sandaruwan who has disciplined both his mind and body to near perfection, decides not to brood anymore. Yet he allows, "Such thoughts to take over his life completely, like a creeper that slowly wrapped itself around a giant tree and then slowly smothered it completely" (102).

In his third role / life, now, he chooses a life of simplicity, opting an appropriate name Chandare, a common name, meaning a moon. Accepting a self-composed life, like 'the moon', serene in glory, he decides: "not to desire or yearn for anything beyond him, to long for things unattainable" (107). As his stream of consciousness goes, "Chandare was Romiel. A younger Romiel in a worn out pair of shorts instead of a loin cloth, living on a coconut plantation, instead of a small vegetable plot". "Romiel was the son of Chandare, Chandare was the son of Sandaruwan. Sandaruwan was the son of Chandranatne. Chandranatne was the son of Romiel" (106).

The narrator concludes the novel connoting a chief philosophical basis of Buddhist thought. Dissanayake's mind that contemplates Buddhism, readily conceives new ideas. He is skillful in presenting not only the impeccable but startling ideas, connected with technology and science. His novel, "Moonstone", depicts the strange life of a protagonist who is prepared to commit\ a parricide to meet his ideal, his ultimate object of life. He is confident and constant in his attempt to make his father "be reborn", as his own biological son. To pursue his obsession he makes strenuous efforts, calculating the right time of conception and the right time his father should die. But the unexpected demise of his father deprives him of his chances of success. He who is convinced that he is not committing any sin against his father or against society has a strong faith in Gods, who have stayed with him in all his endeavors. But finally he realises that his blindness of ignorance has prevented him from seeing his actions as they really are. Dissanayake concludes his novel with an astounding revelation that it is ignorance or delusion that makes us believe the impermanent as permanent and the unreal as real. Sandaruwan whose mind has got befuddled with his obsession, on his realisation becomes serene. Becoming free from guilt, with a clear conscience, he achieves his victory. He succeeds by accepting life as it is and by his decision not to long for things unattainable.

Works Cited

Primary Source: www.Saadhu.com.daya@saadhu.com

en.m.wikipedia.org.

www.researchgate.net

Regi Siriwardena upon examination of "Miracle under Kumbuk Tree" In *conversation with Daya Dissanayake* – Jayadeep Sarangi:

Writers in conversation vol.6 Nos. 1 Feb.2019.

CHAPTER 4

Regression in Daya Dissanayake's *Miracle under Kumbak Tree*

X. Anita Arul

Life is a package of emotions and feelings. It has to move on. Every minute detail may sometimes lead to arguing and end up with unexpected results that may not be rectified. We are very much conscious to keep up our ego. Sometimes the mask that we wear to hide our originality from the society means a lot. But when it exceeds the limit it damages and spoils the entire scenario. The entire fence that we build around us inorder to safeguard us from all the pricking pains, false accusations, fear, guilt, anxiety help us to function without getting affected mentally.

Due to pressurised commitment that an individual faces from the family, friends, relatives and society the self-suppress the reality and it is gladdened to expose the fake faces. The inefficient voices undergo painful remarks and their external egoistic attitude strongly deprives their real existence with real feelings. There a kind of acting and hiding of emotions take place. The defense mechanism they use eventually helps them to protect from all the vulnerabilities that aim to destroy them. Apparently, when it goes beyond its limit that may cause some serious effects that may bind rightfully the progress of an individual.

Psychological trauma takes a person to any extreme that he digresses from the path he travels and ended up in exhibiting the suppressed emotions to cope up with the circumstances. Behavior of a person matters a lot in the society. When something overturned or disordered with any such commitment and the unsolvable matters are psychologically dealt within the mind. An individual get hurts and that sticks to the mind and disturbs the entire protocol. It can be released only if it is defended by any sheet that compensates the humiliations they undergo. Detached attitude from any of such frustration may not be helpful for the person to come out off the problem they face in every walk of life. Some poignant moments may not be entirely eradicated from the mind of the affected individual instead it stays in the unconscious mind and it essayed like nothing can repay the painful moments.

Imprisoned with the thoughts that eat up the mind is never going to be a fruitful one. It is absolutely going to collapse the whole system of any institution like relationships between individuals and with the society. To keep us always in the light it is not the right way to keep everyone in the dark. Decades and decades the engaged part may not give any kind of positivity in the work and automatically results in swirling vortex of revenge towards the one who made the emotions get triggered. Everyone marches towards successful stories. When the shadowy powers prevent those obstacles a kind of battle goes within the mind where a need of an earnest solution arises. The emotional chord when touched will lead to muddle up the right to life. In Daya's "Miracle under the Kumbuk Tree" the protagonist of the novel, Babli who is from a village background and one whose parents are ignorant of things apart from their village. The village is their world. Babli is trying to cope up with the situations empowering herself. When that is not so protective Babli uses the defense mechanism regression inorder to keep herself dominant overpowering her incapable situations.

Inequality in the society, victimisation, self-blaming, trauma, misplaced maternal love, and feeling of shame, self-doubt and hurt that cannot be explained must be encountered so Babli, the protagonist finds a way of life altering. She undergoes many problems right from her childhood or even from her early stage of her life. Babli is a very silent personality who never reveals anything about her to anyone in her office. No one is aware of her past life or even the present. "Babli was a mystery to everyone in the office. They could not get anything out of her about her family, her home-town or her school. She did not get any phone calls. She did not receive any letters."

Babli is suspected to have been suffering from Asperger's Syndrome because she doesn't have any socialising sense with her fellow workers. She neither communicates nor maintains any kind of relationship too. She has her own way of life. Her childhood is not mentionable. She faces lot of miseries during that period. Babli "was the most unfortunate girl on earth and no one had ever suffered like her". (10) She is the one who would never like anyone to taste this bitter experience as she has undergone during her childhood. It is in her unconscious mind and it makes her feel inferior too. Suffering, struggle, defeat have become a part and parcel of her life. These people normally will be known well about life and Babli is also not an exception to it. A sensitivity, compassion and love develop within them and concern towards others can also be seen.

In this novel "*Miracle under Kumbuk Tree*", Babli is reserved to the people around that she never explicates her feelings to others. She associates rain with her sad and gloomy part of life. She is the one who haven't acknowledged any peace at home while growing up. The words that provoked her to feel the spirit of loss lingers in her psyche though she grows bigger. "Father would walk away saying, 'the two of you will be the death of me' (11). She permits some glimpses enter into her world once in a while comprehending the benefits by using the defense mechanism regression. It is told that whosoever approves with regression beyond its line may suffer to the core. During depression and distressed situation this psychological mechanism which is so strange is unknowingly taken in hand to bring back the strength and stability.

For Babli it's a miracle that happened to get a chance for her to go to school. She met with a fire accident and admitted at the hospital. Her father came to see her with a plastic doll. It is the only present brought by her father ever she could sense the love of her father for the first time in her life. So wherever she goes she will be with the doll that takes her to the childhood, love and the memories of her father.

> The plastic doll had been with her ever since. The little doll her father had brought her when he came to the hospital to see her. The only toy, the only present, she had ever got from her father. Or that is what she had believed till she realised that the greatest gift he had given her was the strength to love him and her mother in spite of everything (13)

Babli's love towards her father is immeasurable. She decides to kill herself for the sake of her father's life. She cannot disappear from her place too, that is from earth too. She never used to have any conversation with her father, Eddie. The traumatic pasts or the loss of happiness portray clearly the pain that followed Babli all through her life. "The two of you will be the death of me", (21) describes the emotional descriptions that Babli would have passed through in her childhood.

Babli's early childhood in the coconut estate is her better days in her lifetime because that is the time she sees her father and mother quite normal before they get addicted to liquor. Babli always holds a kind of fear for her father as she is not quite sure about his mood. He will be bursting into anger sometimes and he might be in good mood at times. She always return to this unscathed physically when grown up and eventually end up in regression. The pain that interlaced with her life affects her and when she indulges in activities she could not be active and so endearing that the strange flavours of discomfort tenanted Babli.

When Babli wants to get detached from the harsh reality related to her father's illness, heart transplant she began to day dream thinking of her life as a student and her life in the estate where they were thrown out off the place. The abandonment that caused to them stays in the mind of Babli despite her success in her lifeline. She wants to achieve things in a harmless way bigger than the estate owner. A spiraling dream in her mind was like spreading some powerful judgment towards the estate owner's atrocity towards them.

> She would go to the estate in a newer and bigger car than the one the cruel man owned. Then her imagination had turned to the way the cruel man had fallen. How the man had become poor, had sold his car, had sold his house in the city and had become as poor as Babli herself had been. (43)

Babli's habit of day dreaming helped her to ornate herself and especially to have a sound sleep when she struggles to sleep. The thought of morality gave her peace of mind. Babli whenever she feels bad, apparently fear of things, whenever she feels that she is left aloof posing a kind of loneliness she cuddles up with her doll. The unaccepted facts or reality is not able to be faced by her and so this way of going back is used by her which will help her for a metamorphic change. Babli is struggling in her life to lead a double-sided life "like a frog that was at ease in water or land…she at times felt that she should never have left the water to try the life on dry land" (49). Her unattainability in some aspects makes her depressed in the contemporary context. She tries to figure out the issues and fix the stolen happiness in small things around.

Babli receives no proper or remarkable favour from her parents. this encompasses a possibly merging attitude with herself without expecting aid unnecessarily from others. When Babli is beaten up by her father she often feels frustrated and the thought that highlighted in her mind is with umpteen numbers of questions that she doubts whether they are her real parents. "Babli wondered how any mother could forget such an important moment in their lives, the birth of the only child." (59). All these lead her to be in darkness. She is trying to explore herself amidst the light of trauma. Her birth identity is always pointed out with huge insults. The chord that holds things together is shaken when she is traced of her parentage. The early abuse and negligence vastly influenced her that she undergoes a battle within representing her as a powerful soul inspite of many dark realities. She suppresses all these brutal things in her unconscious mind and used to recall the first doll that her father bought her during the time of accident. She throws a kind of ripples, "Babli did not want to look at her mother. Her anger towards her parents and the pain of frustration burned her insides, so was numb to everything else around her" (60). She has created a complex inner self and to escape from this day dream about her childhood days as well as about her futuristic vision hold her and gives her support.

Babli is a girl with dreams in her heart and mind. She wishes to take her parents in a vehicle and when the possibility becomes a question she goes to day dream to get a new own car and to take her parents on pilgrimage. She processes the emotions and makes it stay at the back of mind. She is willing to explain to her father the miracles of the Bo Tree but the conversation between them are not so meaningful or lengthy moreover it is clear that they don't converse with each other. She has an earnest thirst to share many things with her father. Her mind at times goes to hatred mode as she was so scared of her father during her early miserable childhood. Feeling less about oneself is a curse and psychologically when the defense mechanism is used as a shield it helps the person to heal the individual to an extent.

The unintentional return to the past because of the shame and hurt is inevitable as it is a part of human condition. Facing unsolvable problems, desires not gratified during childhood daily make Babli get upset with things around. She often travels back carrying memorable events in order to get back to normal mood. Childish behavior of having doll with her "It is with her. She holds it to her chest when she goes to sleep. She keeps it with her on the table when she studies. She used to keep it in her school bag when she was a child" (90) and going back to past recalling some incidents can be a temporary relief for Babli. Later in her life time she became aware of some truth regarding life and started come out of brooding and tries to help her father in coming out of depression and starts treatment too. Babli too comes closer to nature and she is away from false memories too. Though the relationship between father Eddie and Babli is stubborn "the bond, a paternal umbilical cord, would have been there always, invisible and dormant till today, till this moment." (99)

Works Cited

Dissanayake, Daya. *Miracle under the Kumbuk Tree.* Sarasvi Publishers (Pvt.) Ltd, 2012. Print

CHAPTER 5

Daya Dissanayake's *Moonstone*: An Inner Journey towards Consciousness

Anju S. Nair

> "*Annica vata* sankhara. Everything in this world is impermanent. We live in an ever-changing world, while we ourselves are changing."

The human ideal is exemplified in the words of Hamlet, "What a piece of work is man! How noble in reason! How infinite in faculty!

Scholasticism ushered in an era of rational thought which led to several scientific inventions that opened man's eyes to the unexplored realms of the universe. While geographical discoveries revealed the existence of new lands and other cultures, there was an urge to question the traditional. With the advent of modernism there was an earnest concern for the new realities of human life and a desire to recreate it. In writing, the writers manipulated plot and language to create new narratives that defy chronology and clear-cut interpretations. The Sri Lankan writer Daya Dissanayake's novel "*Moonstone*" is concerned with the response of man in the face of situations that compel an individual to make a moral choice. The protagonist of the novel, Sandaruwan has a fantastic conception of himself – he thinks he is infinite. Sandaruwan was a billionaire businessman, living on his own little island. His father was still living the life of a poor farmer, all alone in a remote village in Sri Lanka. Sandaruwan was obsessed with the idea that he had to look after his father and provide him with the same luxurious life. Sandaruwan decides the best way is to get his father to be born as his own son.

The development takes place in the mind of the protagonist with the philosophical concept of rebirth that influences him. As rightly said by Tagore, the "mind has its necessity also. It must find out reason in things. It is faced with a multiplicity of facts, and is bewildered when it cannot find one unifying principle which simplifies the heterogeneity of things". (3)The mind makes him believe that he can achieve the anything because of this infinite state. He presumes he possesses a pure abstract will and has condescension towards the average. Sandaruwan liked to think of the "period before he left for the United States as his previous birth."(5) To him, "Home was only the house where his father lived. That was all. It was not home for him". (6)

Sandaruwan perceives with a degree of controlled thought for he is aware of his inner state. His actions are marked by thought, will, design and critical awareness. His concerns are manifested by strong feelings and notions. But he is concerned excessively with himself. He seeks his own advantage, pleasure and well-being without regard for others. "He controlled his vast empire from where he lived and had his most permanent residence, in a small island off La Digue in the Seychelles, where he lived and worked most of the time. Thanshana.com was truly a global business empire and a true example of a global business village. Sandaruwan believed that he could run his business more efficiently and more effectively from this room in his house, than by personally going to the other offices."(13)

Sandaruwan is far more interested in the physical aspects of the world around him than in its social or emotional aspects. Sandaruwan's lifestyle was similar to the lifestyle of the rich and the famous. His residence and office was well sufficient in many other ways. "He had a hybrid system of solar panels and several wind turbines which gave him uninterrupted power for all the needs of his office, home and estate. Water, was pumped from a deep well, purified and used for drinking and cooking. Water for all other purpose was recycled …He did not have visitors. He has not believed in holding regular parties or dinners, and had them only when necessary, either to entertain some of his visiting business associates, or close friends from overseas. (15) The visitors commented that his residence is "what a paradise would be like". (16) Most of the people were of the opinion that Sandaruwan was a really lucky man. But they did not know his perturbed inner self, of his obsession about his father. The thoughts of his father leading an extremely simple life in his village continued to haunt him. He could not concentrate on his work, because images of his father seemed to appear continuously leaving him anxious and restless. He tried to resist, but past memories of his father were dragging him away from his work. The images pursued him and he is taken back to the past. The resisting force – "some contrary force in itself" – stands for the occasional efforts taken by man amidst the monotonous flow of existence. In his backward motion towards the source, man most shows what he is. In the act of revisiting he realises his full potential as a human being. "Sandaruwan spent hours on the roof top of his mansion living the various lives."(35) In the backward motion of the mind running counter to itself the writer sees the origin of all human beings.

By performing something extraordinary that calls for courage and heroism man attains self-realisation and it is this that makes life worthwhile. The spirit of the human race is exhibited in this resistance of the usual flow of the stream of existence and it is from this that man derives his special quality. Sandaruwan wants to do something inconceivable. He contemplates on rebirth. The search for information on rebirth confirmed his belief that nothing was impossible with the modern technology available. "The last moment of consciousness belonging to the immediately previous life, causes the arising of the first moment of consciousness of the next birth."(38)

The state of constant flux of existence is compared with the movement of a chariot wheel. "When it is rolling, touches the ground at one point only of the circumference of the tire, so too of living beings lasts only for a single conscious moment. When that consciousness has ceased, the being is said to have ceased. We have come to one particular moment of death, which marks the end of existence. We should not be distressed by it. Life will continue in the next existence, dying every moment."(39) But this is a deception for existence according to Lucretian theory is in a perpetual state of flux and it moves towards death and nothingness, except as somehow resisted by the spirit of human beings. Sandaruwan's determined mind drives him to achieve the impossible and he begins to contemplate on rebirth by moving one step further. He wanted his father to be reborn as his own son and wanted to make him the luckiest father in the world, in his next birth. "If rebirth was possible, then it should not be difficult to find out the time and place of the new birth. Then it should be possible to create a situation where the new time and place of birth could be controlled. Each event was the result of a previous event or action. If the actions could be monitories and controlled the reaction could be predetermined."(40) Sandaruwan started reading many article on rebirth and in one article there was a reference to cloning, but all his research into rebirth did not give him a satisfactory answer "about the possible link of a cloned human being to past birth."(52) His father's clone would be like his father's brother, not Sandaruwan's son. He considered a human clone to be "a total confusion in society, in law and in astrology."(53)

Dissanayaka's vision is a moral one. He sees life as a struggle between right and wrong or rather between good and evil. The world is incurably corrupt. To be involved in it is to be inescapably involved in evil; all its apparent beauties are a snare and delusion. Ambition, pleasure, beauty, passion, the lust of the eyes and the pride of life – to look at these for happiness is to be certain of disappointment and disillusionment. "Sandaruwan had disciplined both his mind and body to near perfection. It was the secret of his success. He had been able to compartmentalise his mind and his thoughts and his work, and had developed the ability to shut the door completely to anyone of more of such compartments. Thus we knew that he could have easily shut off all his thoughts of his father, as easily as he had done everything else. Sandaruwan did not have to think of his father. Yet he had allowed such thoughts to take over his life completely, like a creeper that slowly wrapped itself around a giant tree and then slowly smothered it completely."(102) throughout the novel Sandaruwan's attention centers on his father, on his relationship with him, on his business empire he had built, and on the other physical elements of his surroundings.

The writer has exposed the selfishness and behavior of the big guns of society, who seldom pay any heed to the cries of the poor and the vulnerable. The novelist interprets the truth, through the character of the protagonist who represents the reality of life. To look at him is to look at life. To know him is to know the truth. The writer gives us profound insight into human existence and maladies that endanger the individual, the community and humanity as a whole.

"The world of science is not a reality; it is an abstract world of force. We can use it by the help of our intellect but cannot realise it by the help of our personality. It is like a swarm of mechanics that though producing things for ourselves as personal beings, are mere shadows to us. But there is another world which is real to us. We can see it, feel it; deal with it with all our emotions. Its mystery is endless because we cannot analyse it or measure it. We can but say, here you are." (Tagore 4)Towards the end of the novel the protagonist is drawn towards the world of reality. Sandaruwan had always boasted that "he had a very clear and analytical mind that he could always get right to the bottom of any problem, on the issue of the rebirth of his father he had been blinded by his own craving, his own *thanha*, that his desire to find a solution had distracted him from the Truth." (114)

Hence the end of the novel shows the beginning of experience. It is also a comment on the need for survival and the idea that nature limits human achievement, is most explicit. The novel is an examination of the legend of the tough modern self-centered man and his innate superiority. Sandaruwan slowly "came to a realisation that what he had attempted to do was clearly impossible." (114)

The protagonist Sandaruwan, takes a journey in his mind, and moves backwards and forwards from an exalted opinion of himself to realising that he is a mere mortal. His self-centeredness and limitations are seen from the beginning of the novel. He has an excess of the affluent attitude which finally results in his dreams being shattered. He mistakes his lovelessness and lack of contact as detachment. He continues to recognise in himself a genius which is simply not there. His conception of himself was very high and so his trying period was more and he experiences the pain in his inner journey. The philosophy is the idea that human life has no redeeming meaning or purpose. The only certain thing in life is the inevitability of death, and because all humans will eventually meet death, all lives are equally meaningless. Sandaruwan finally realises that just as he is indifferent to much of the universe, so is the universe indifferent to him.

Dissanayaka depicts his protagonist Sandaruwan as a representative of humanity. He offers the central concept of Sandaruwan's career as the need to strive. This alone would entitle him to eternal salvation. Sandaruwan is a many splendored personality who is highly controversial in his attitudes, bahaviour and principles. The age in which he lived is the postmodern age, yet the old values and attitudes persisted among his fellow men, well portrayed through the father.

Moonstone is an interesting and elusive novel. It is realistic and fantastic. All the incidents seem to take place in the physical and the mental world and this lends ambiguity to the novel. The novel is a complex work of idealism removed from the human conflict of conscience and love. It shows the awful consequences of a man's deliberate commitment to himself with a view to gratifying his pride and his ambition.

Works Cited

Dissanayake, Daya. *Moonstone.* Sarasavi Publishers. 2006. Print

Das, Sisir Kumar. *The English Writings of Rabindranath Tagore.* Vol 3. Sahitya Academi. 1999. Print.

CHAPTER 6

Capsulisation of Euthenics in Daya Dissanayake's *The Healer and the Drug Pusher*

J. Miraclin and M.Beula Hemalatha

Euthenics is a branch of art and science that deals with the improvement of human functioning, efficiency, and well-being by modifying controllable environmental factors such as living conditions and education. The word euthenics is derived from the Greek word "euthenein" which means, to "thrive or flourish". The word euthenics was established by Ellen Swallow Richards (1842-1911) in her book The Cost of Shelter (1905). She used the word euthenics to mean "The science of better living". In 1927, Technology Week went on to define euthenics as "man's environmental opportunity," "his education". Daya's *The Healer and the Drug Pusher* published in 2000 ignites the idea of improving humankind and human functioning by the concept of modifying controllable conditions, such as better shelter, efficient living, and education.

Daya Dissanayake, through the novel, *The Healer and the Drug Pusher* tends to inculcate traditional ideas and ancient medicinal practices that have been followed and practised by our ancestors to heal the patients and to lead a robust and healthy life. The novel also discusses the terrifying changes in the medication methods and well-being of mankind within a thousand years. The author explicitly talks about the changes in the preferences of people within centuries and the drugs they consume without second thought. As drugs that are prescribed by doctors provide immediate and satisfying results, people favour the advanced methods of healing and have lost interest in traditional methods.

The author urges to revive the traditional and ancient practices that don't harm mankind as it doesn't have any side effects. He believes that the revival of such traditional practices would help mankind to escape from the harmful effects of drugs, manufactured by multi-national companies.

Bhanu, the daughter of Raju Tavapalan is against her own father who markets pharmaceuticals. She states that "Doctor's prescription drugs kill more people than from tobacco and alcohol" (13). The author depicts Bhanu as a rebellious person who desperately opposes the drugs and the manufacturing companies that make "big profits from it" (13). She is acquainted with the harmful side effects of the drugs that her father sells. She blames Raju for offering the drugs to doctors who "offer the zero option" (13) to their patients. She claims that "the drugs are more harmful because they are sold and purchased openly" (13).

Bhanu is portrayed as a young girl in the 20th century who is bothered about the well-being of the people around her. She tries to dissuade Raju from marketing pharmaceuticals that kills people without their knowledge. Bhanu claims that "smooth is not safe". It destroys liver tissue. It should never have been introduced to this country. It is better to live with acne, than die from liver failure."(61). Eventually Bhanu wins the argument as the company decides to stop manufacturing 'smooth' that damages the liver tissues of the body. But Raju knows that "their company had already planned a new campaign to market several of the existing products under new brand names, with a slight change in the composition, but at much higher prices."(134).

By the Act of wearing a T-shirt that says 'Say no to Drugs', she seems to encourage the traditional methods of medication and opposes the consumption of harmful drugs that are being prescribed to the people who are unaware of its side effects. The author, thereby, warns the readers to abandon the advanced healing methods and to embrace our ancient methods that have been taught by our ancestors.

Our ancestors made use of the naturally available herbs and plants to cure the patients. They found that it does no harm and is the simple remedy to relieve a patient from physical and mental infirmity as well. Moreover, the companies manufacture drugs in order to make money is not demanded by our ancestors to cure a patient.

Minda, a fisherman in Tamil village of Jaffna and his son Kita set out to the sea for fishing where they find Mitra in an abandoned boat. Minda takes him to the shore and an elderly man diagnoses the stranger and says that his skin is peeling because of salt and sunburn. Ramu, a villager brings two banana leaves, a plank of wood from his front door. The stranger is lifted on the banana leaves and is taken to the hospital which is a part of Buddhist monastery. They are told that the stranger had lost his eyesight and has become blind. Minda says if the physicians need "some special herbs or materials for the preparation of medicines, I will tell them that we will search for the things" (12).

The Mahawedna begins the immersion therapy to cure his sunburnt skin and bring down his fever. The cavity of the bath is half-moon shaped and is "filled with a herbal preparation of sour gruel made from boiled with alcohol, milk, ghee and whey" (21). The Mahawedna also teaches his students to cure the patients with herbs, gruel and explains substitute ingredients which could be used when certain ingredients are not available. "If milk is not available, you can make a decoction of aralu, bavila, sirivedi bavila and undu" (21). Before immersing into the bath he is placed on the stone slab and "Sesame oil and sour milk was applied all over his body" (22).

After gaining eyesight, Mitra and Pali decide to join in a medical college to learn medicine. Mitra says, "I want to learn all I can about treating eye ailments, so that I could help other people like me, who have gone blind. I know what it is to be blind, and so I want to save as many people from this fate" (123).

When Raju was younger, he never wanted to study medicine. He wanted to join in Plantation Corporation but by chance, he began to market pharmaceuticals. Accepting the suggestion made by his headmaster Raju met Mr. Gunaseelan who wanted to hire some young men for marketing pharmaceuticals. He was selected for the job only on the basis of IQ test which was set by a supplier in UK. He tried to persuade his father Thangaraja by stating that "Pharmaceuticals industry is doing a service to mankind" (30). The job of Raju is to tell the doctors "all the advantages of their products and make them believe that they are the most wonderful drugs ever invented to save mankind from extinction." (30). When he learns that Smooth is the cause for Suneeta's illness, he is not ready to take the responsibility. Indeed he gives an evasive answer "we didn't force her to use this product" and thus backs up the products of the company he works for. But eventually, he agrees with his daughter's view on medication but he is aware that nothing can stop the companies from manufacturing the harmful drugs and thereby, killing people every day without their knowledge.

Bhanu charges Raju that Suneeta's illness is due to "Smooth" – the drug launched by the company that Raju works for. Bhanu says "You are trying to murder innocent people" (61). She argues that the money her father earns is "filthy lucre" (62). When Banu tries to persuade her father not to market drugs and articulates its harmful effects. Rather Raju mocks her by saying "don't say such silly things to anyone outside this family, it will show how ignorant you are, about the world around you" (13). But apparently, throughout the novel, the author implies that it is Raju who is ignorant of the side-effects of the drugs he sells and his company's greediness to earn money and selfishness that kills innocent people who consume the drugs that doctors prescribe all around the world.

The conversation between Bhanu and Gunadasa reveals the truth and reality about doctors in 20th century. Bhanu reads the article that says "less people die when doctors are on strike" (64). Moreover, Mr. Gunadasa, uncle of Suneeta has confronted money hungry doctors and thus, Gunadasa believes "the less you see of doctors, the healthier you can be" (64). Gunadasa who has confronted money hungry doctors in his life, declares that "Health depends on prevention, through hygiene and nutrition, not on doctors. Doctors make sick people get worse" (64). He states that doctors who rely on western medicine were money hungry even before two thousand years and they "learnt a little medicine and practised it because they were greedy for wealth" (66). Bhanu backs him up with her statement "I read that people are born healthy and would remain healthy, if their lives are not tampered with, by doctors" (64). The future of euthenics will have a direct impact on health care. Improvement of human functioning can be attainable by providing education about diseases. Therefore, if the population is made aware of inheritable traits that are undesirable and detrimental to health and quality of life, then perhaps those people may be convinced not to reproduce if they possess those traits, thereby preventing them from being passed on.

Through the novel, Daya Dissanayake attempts to create knowledge about different types of medication and wants people to recognise the importance of traditional medical practices that were gifted to mankind by our ancestors. According to Daya, human beings should make use of the naturally available herbs, plants to lead a healthy life. In the 10th century, people were healthy because of the food they consumed and were entirely dependent on naturally available sources. They cooked green leaves and herbs that never harm but strengthen their body. The author also introduces some healthy and medicinal herbs "can you pluck some agatti flowers. We can cook them for dinner and if you pluck some leaves we can have with it rice tomorrow" (49) and Pali explains Mitra about the medicinal qualities of agate "at the hospital they would have used this leaf and bark in some of the medicines they applied on your skin" (49). Even if people fell ill, they head to the hospital, where a patient is cured by the ancient methods of healing and thus the people don't suffer from any side effects.

The author explores the differences in lifestyle of people within a thousand years and shows that people nowadays blindly follow the advanced medication methods and food consumption. The author, throughout the novel, tends to inculcate his ideas to the younger generation about the harmful effects of drugs that people consume without hesitation. In the novel, Bhanu, a young girl is aware of the harmful effects of the drugs that doctors prescribe and thus argues with Raju in order to stop him from selling those drugs and killing innocent people. The author emphasises the need to create awareness among youngsters, by whom mankind can be redeemed from the advanced medicines manufactured by multinational companies.

Daya Dissanayake's *The Healer and the Drug Pusher* is the need of the hour which could bring awareness and changes in the minds of the readers. In this magnum opus of Daya, the philosophy of domestication and urbanisation has within its scope the consideration of the most vital problems affecting the future of the race. More specifically, euthenics seeks to secure the best environmental influence for the physical, mental and moral development of the individual, particularly the young, and for the maintenance of health and vigour especially under modern industrial city conditions.

Works Cited

Dissanayake, Daya. *The Healer and the Drug Pusher.* October 18, 2000.

Bennett, J.H (1983). *Natural selection, heredity, and eugenics.* New York: Clarendon Press.

Carlson, E. (2001). *The Unfit: A History of a Bad Idea.* New York: Cold Spring Harbor Laboratory Press.

CHAPTER 7

Miracle under the Kumbak Tree: A Review Article

Renu Milind Dhotre

Miracle under the Kumbak Tree by Daya Dissanayake is set in a small village in modern day Sri Lanka. Sri Lanka is an island country in South East Asia, surrounded on all sides by the Indian Ocean. Most of the country men follow either Buddhism or Hinduism. As per Hindu mythology, this land was ruled by Ravana, who kidnapped Sita, the wife of Ram. Ravana was eventually defeated by Ram on his quest to save his wife. Sri Lanka's geographic location and deep harbours have made it a strategic location which led to colonisation first by Portuguese, then Dutch and then the British. After attaining independence from the British, Sri Lanka was subjected to a civil war which ended in 2009 post the decisive victory of the Sri Lankan Armed Forces over the Liberation Tigers of Tamil Eelam.

Today, it is a developing country and the socio-economic condition of the people has improved a lot in the last decade owing to political stability, stringent laws, better governance and adoption of technology. The country folk are seeing a new way of life and being creatures of habit; seem averse to all the changes happening around them. Thanks to it being a major port on the silk route, Sri Lanka enjoys people from diverse backgrounds and ethnic groups and this has led to a multinational state, with the majority of Sinhalese folks.

Daya Dissanayake is a Sri Lankan author who writes in English as well as Sinhalese. He has many publications to his name, fiction and non-fiction both, spanning across novels, a collection of poems and literary articles. One of his famous works include, 'Who is Ashoka?', a critical review on King Ashoka from the Maurya dynasty. Dissanayake's work spans across Sri Lankan sentiments, subtly bringing about the most obvious but easy to miss perceptions. His books are an easy read, written in simple language for the common man, to read and absorb. He is an acclaimed award winning contemporary author in Sri Lanka.

Miracle under the Kumbak Tree is an emotional moment between the protagonist, Babli and her father, Eddie and is believed to be a turning point for the protagonist's family. Babali is a young girl, but she has inherited all the motherly instincts as a future mother to be, who would be practicing Brahma Vihara, Metta, karuna, Mudita, Upeksha. "She watched her father from a distance, heard his laughter, with a pride probably a mother would have for a young son. After the miracle, they were bathing at the tank after hard days of work in the garden. Her love for her father comes naturally to her. She was a child of Mother Earth. I am a child of this soil. I want to feel it; I want to let Mother Earth caress my feet. She had once told the priest at the church. The life-long strained relationship between the father and daughter is healed under the Kumbak tree and along with it, Eddie is cured of the life-threatening heart disease, miraculously, and has a second chance at life. The healing of Eddie's ailment is considered a miracle because the only medicines that he was taking were supposed to be sustaining his current state and not causing any improvement. He was not taking any alternate medicine either. However, after the moment at the Kumbak tree, Eddie sees fast recovery miraculously. He is entirely healed of his ailment and also of his alcoholism, another habit he had all through his adult life.

The author explores many topics in the book ranging from life in a Sri Lankan Village, life of a daily laborer, the rampant inequality, teachings of Buddhism & Christianity, psychological impact of a broken home, importance of Education, work of missionaries, alcoholism, filial bond, suicide, meditation and places of worship in and across Sri Lanka. While the book is an easy read, the vast array of topics makes it very reflective and a lot has been kept open to interpretation.

The book is quite traditional in its style in the sense that it starts very cryptically in sad and mysterious circumstances and later on, one by one the mystery is unfolded and the story ends on a happy note. Babli's father was critical and in need of a heart transplant as per his doctors and initial medical. While the Christian missionary was willing to aid with the transplant cost, they had to wait for finding a human heart for the transplant. Feeling helpless, Babli decides to take matters in her own hands by attempting suicide and hoping they find her in a good enough condition to use her heart for the transplant.

It was a stroke of luck that her good natured behavior and regular routine led to the landlady figuring out something was amiss and helped save her life. Damien, her employer, who seems to be quite influential in Colombo, plays a huge role in saving Babli's life initially and later on providing support to help her with time and resources for her father's recovery. Babli refused all monetary support from Damien, however, she knew that support was available if she ever required it. The story seems to build a connection between Babli and her employer, but doesn't quite complete it. Background on Damien is missing, and one could help but think maybe the connection between Damien and Babli would eventually lead to friendship or a relationship or if it was only an overt act of support from an employer to the employee. The latter also begets the question if the employer would provide similar support if any other employee was in Babli's place and undergoing similar predicament.

Babli grew in extreme poverty in a village near Chilaw in the north western province of Sri Lanka. Both her parents were daily wage workers, addicted to alcohol, of the illicit kind that is brewed in villages, more harmful than the ones imported from western countries. The author shed some light on the history of alcohol, intoxication, alcoholism and its effect on people. The book ends Eddie's miseries once he stops drinking alcohol, thus making author's opinion on the same very clear. Prior to alcohol addiction, Eddie's family was comparatively happy. Eddie did not like alcohol and did not consume in his early days.

The addiction began when Eddie started working and realised that on pay day irrespective of him drinking or abstaining, he still had to pay for the after part. To him, it seemed a waste of his hard earned money and he started par-taking in the same with his fellow workers. Later, he met Jayartane, a coconut plucker, whose influence turned this monthly enjoyment into daily addiction and when Eddie was addicted, Jayaratne demanded payment for alcohol. As he didn't have any money to pay, he took Jayaratne's offer and allowed him to steal coconuts to sell from the estate that Eddie was guarding. News soon reached the estate owner and Eddie and his family was kicked out of the estate, left to fend for themselves without any home or resources.

Eddie's family sought refuge with Jayaratne and Jayaratne tried to teach Eddie coconut plucking. When that didn't work, he involved him in hi illicit liquor business. However, Jayaratne's liquor business was soon raided by the police and he was jailed. Jayaratne eventually lost his life in jail. It was by a stroke of luck that Eddie wasn't with Jayaratne on the day of raid and was saved. Later on, Eddie's family continued living in Jayaratne's home and land; neighbors unaware of their backgrounds.

While they had a place to stay, Eddie's family was primarily unskilled and getting by was extremely difficult. Babli's parents would seek outdoor work and with the meagre wages they would earn, part of it was spent on Eddie's alcohol. Slowly, her mother started drinking as well and there were times that no food was cooked in the house, especially when Babli grew up and started working in Colombo. Both her parents would spend the day drinking.

Growing up, Babli had a strained relationship with her father. While he loved her, he wanted a son, who would look after him in old age and accepting the same from a daughter was very difficult for him. He would have preferred living in an old age home than accepting help from her own daughter. However, this changed thanks in part to Sudu Banda, the wise old school master, who helped reach out to Eddie and helped him open up.

Families in Sri Lankan villages use bottle lamps for light at night as electricity is still not accessible to everyone. Once there was an incident and Babli was badly burnt, however this was another time when she got lucky as her father was home and he rescued her and found transportation fairly quickly to the nearby hospital. Being a bottle lamp burn victim, Babli came under the radar of Timothy Foundation, a Christian missionary, that stepped up to help her. Eventually in the days that passed, they ensured that her house was re-built, she was admitted in a school and also get all her identity documents. Her mother tried to take undue advantage of her burns by trying to show her urns and beg in the market. Foundation had to intervene and stop this, which helped avoid any further embarrassment to Babli.

Schooling opened up a new world for her where she was introduced to newer things and was able to meet people who would answer her questions and encourage her to explore and form her own thought process. This helped open avenues for her in the future. Education also helped Babli get through her difficult childhood as she was engrossed in studies and hence didn't end up like her parents. Author has subtly highlighted how education can change not only the individual but an entire family's life. Babli was a brilliant student and thanks to the Asperger's syndrome, she was able to fully concentrate on what she was doing and excel at it.

Her education also helped her understand that while missionaries like Timothy foundation exist to help the under-privileged children like her, they all have political agendas. The kind of funding they received could easily help revolutionise the villages in the vicinity; however, they held back and helped only those in absolute need or who approached them or when it suited them. Babli was not exactly religious, but she believed in the existence of God; she would visit the Buddhist temples and Christian churches out of longing for belongingness than for anything else. The author has also very clearly highlighted how faith, religion and way of life are three different concepts and just because a person prays or visits a church / temple doesn't necessarily mean that he believes in their teachings or would lead his / her life as per the preaching of that religion.

Through Babli's example, the author has tried to show that in their darkest times, people like to hold on to the belief that there is a greater being and when things spin out of control, you can trust him to bring an order to the chaos. The plot reminds me of a dialogue from Game of Thrones, a televised, book series by George. R. R. Martin, that the common man doesn't care for who sits on the throne. All he wishes and prays for is for health and food for his children.

The book also touches on the topic of parental influence and how much parents' behavior affects their children. The unhappy married life of Babli's parents led her to believe that her own marriage might end in a similar fashion and that she didn't want to suffer at the hands of her husband like her mother did. She never considers getting married or even exploring any kind of relationship, thus stunting her own life in a sense. While not marrying is a choice, not giving oneself an opportunity to explore any kind of relationship for the fear that things will take a wrong turn is absolutely wrong. The thought that ones' parents will live a hundred years and one's family will never change is wishful thinking, and people should always plan and be prepared for any exigency that befalls them.

She is also reminded of the loneliness that she felt growing up, hoe her father was always unavailable o didn't care for her well-being and how her mother had to toil day and night to make her life a little easier. However, as she was unhappy in her own life, there was no space for her to meet the emotional needs of a growing child and as Babli grew, she always felt that her parents did not love her or showered her with affection like other parents did to their kids.

The plot of the story becomes more engaging in the second half. Some parts of the story could have been explored further like the traditional healer, Eddie's background, Babli's friends, the healer who works on natural medicines etc.

There are many plots that do not see closure in the book. For instance, the one where Babli's friend invites her to the wedding. This plot seems completely out of place as neither does she go for the wedding nor does she tell her friend of any of her own intentions. While the intent of the author was to make her family feel accepted from the village community, the plot is really out of place as we have not seen any mention of Babli's friends earlier in the book. She comes across as a lonely character and then suddenly there is a friend from the past. The story of Babli's friends' husband also seems equally irrelevant to the plot. It is unclear what the author was trying to narrate in the whole bit.

Another plot that could have been explored further was how Eddie's two medical reports that are two months apart are vastly different, point of contention being his ill health could also be due to regular alcohol intake and emotional distress; as no other medicine was used for his treatment. The initial set of reports could be erroneous. There was to be a re-examination after the second set of reports to confirm the status of Eddie's heart. While the author wishes to highlight that a clean life-style and faith in God can lead to miracles, the same does not come out very clearly. Another loop hole that is there is Eddie, a life-long addict becomes completely clean in a matter of two months. Similarly, the daughter who lost hope, tried suicide is suddenly resilient and emerges the strongest amongst all the characters. While the plot is sound, the timeline feels rushed.

The central theme of the book lies around education, faith in God and family bonds. Education helps create awareness and family helps keep a person grounded. While Babli follows both Buddhism and Christianity, she is not entirely sure if a greater being exists. However, in times of distress, she takes comfort in the existence of a greater being. She is also reminded time and again of the rampant inequality, however she understands that this is the way of life and there is nothing that can be done about it. Point of commendation for Sri Lanka is that the poverty percentage for people in Sri Lanka has declined by about 5% in the past decade.

Author has also discussed some Buddhist philosophies in the book such as dharma, karma, Bodhi tree etc. Bodhi puja was performed and healing will be based on past karma is assumed. The author has also discussed how Buddhist monks are supposed to sacrifice everything in order to attain nirvana and yet those in politics, would sooner gain political advantage than attaining nirvana.

The book also illustrates the idiom, one can take the horse to the water-source, but one can't feed water to the horse. While the entire village was willing to help Eddie and the family, the steps for reform had to be taken by the family. The book also shows how cautiousness and helpfulness increases once a life threatening situation occurs in someone's family. The same society had left Babli and her family to their condition, however, with the actions of Babli, the society rallied to help the family for its betterment.

The author has highlighted many key issues and touched up on a lot of societal issues. These could have been penned a little more eloquently if not so subtly. The author has also used some Buddhist and Sinhala terms, which have been barely explained in the footnotes, and might appear difficult for a foreign reader to decipher. Overall, the book is a good read, engaging and having scope for readers' imaginations to run wild.

Kumbuk is the Arjun Tree considered sacred in India. It is found in Sri Lanka too by the side of rivers and tanks. It is of significance in this novel because it is a majestic Vanaspathi, it is long lived, and formulations containing the powdered bark have been used for this and other heart conditions for several thousand years along with Tamarind, Myrobalan, Ginger and many other herbs in the preparations to regain the strength of the heart muscles. All this reminds us of the value of our treasured vegetation. Towards the end of the novel, one can evaluate that corruption and disaster could happen even in a remote village but the simple village life and the peaceful natural environment can create miracles. Filial devotion is the main theme of the novel although other sub-themes exist to dominate.

The book doesn't have an ending but a list of options that the protagonist could pursue further, leaving it to the reader's imagination. This also leaves scope for sequel of the book and there are many avenues for a spin-off.

Works Cited

Dissanayake, Daya. *Miracle under the Kumbak Tree.* Sarasavi. Colombo, 2012.

CHAPTER 8

Exploring Ecological Wisdom in Daya Dissanayake's Novel *The Clone*

D. Vijaya Lakshmi

Introduction

In the realm of literature, the study of ecology was a novel perspective that suggested ecological approaches to literature. Ecological thinking appeared in literature in the early nineteenth century but it was recognised in the late twentieth century which means the 1990s. It came into existence with an intention of creating worldwide awareness of the environmental crisis which enhances the relationship between the environment and literature. Poets and writers of the 1990s brought a significant aspect to the human mind that it would be a great threat to humankind and Mother Earth in the future. Due to this reason, writings on ecological wisdom attracted young researchers and they tried identifying the solutions to this crisis.

In this book chapter, the researcher focuses on ecological wisdom in the novel, *The Clone* of Dayananda Dissanayake, a famous Sri Lankan poet, novelist and blogger. His columns appear in newspapers, magazines and other publications and currently, he is one of the most popular Sinhalese authors. He started his journey of writing a debut novel Kat Bitha in 1998 and reached the height of introducing the first e-novel to the readers of Asia. All the books brought various commendations and each book adds feathers in his cap. He is the only Sinhalese writer to receive the Sri Lankan State Literary Award for the best English novel thrice and was awarded in 2013 the SAARC Literary Award.

A theoretical and conceptual framework will certainly help the researchers or readers who may not be familiar with the concepts focused in the present study. Exploring Daya Dissanayake's novel *The Clone* from an ecological perspective requires that the clarification of some concepts and theories that are basic to this issue. The Oxford Dictionary of English gives the definition for wisdom, "wisdom" as "the quality of having experience, knowledge and good judgement." It is one's ability to make good ethical choices. Wisdom is considered a personality trait, which is related to knowledge, whereas the acquisition of knowledge does not guarantee the acquisition of wisdom (Guerell and Riffert, 2011). Norwegian philosopher Arne Naess first put forth the concept of "ecological wisdom" based on his eco-centric personal philosophies, ecosophies, combining the root words from ancient Greek *ecos* (household place) and *sophia* (wisdom) Drengson and Devall 2010). Ecology---the study of the common household ---is about "knowing our home and the relations that live there" (Sewall, 1999, p. 253). Ecologically, reality itself may even be understood to be "the framework of relations with which all appearances tally" (Merleau-Ponty, 2002, 349).

Arne Naess, the Guru of 'Deep Ecology' during the early 1970s, suggested that the environmentalists needed to encourage the people to conserve and to protect the environment. He reiterated that a revolutionary understanding of human nature should be developed to understand the environment as there is deep connection between the human self and nature. According to Naess, the well-being and flourishing of humans and non-humans life on the Earth have prominence in itself and this prominence is self-regulating of the concern of the nonhuman world for human purposes. But the growth of human life and culture is compatible with a substantially smaller human population (Naess, 68). If there is no such concern for human beings on non-humans there is an imbalance between the population of nonhuman and human. It leads to the depletion of flora and fauna. It is well said in Amitav Ghosh's novel, The Hunger Tide, "This Island has to be saved for its trees, it has to be saved for its animals, it is a part of a reserve forest, it belongs to a project to save tigers, which is paid for by people from all around the world (HT, 261)." From Sundarlal Bahuguna's Indian Chipko movement to Wangari Maathai's Kenyan Greenbelt movement, the urge continued to save the environment.

Daya Dissanayake, in his novel, *The Clone*, introduces the readers a lurking disaster that devastates the entire environment. To bring awareness about ecological wisdom to humanity, the author narrates the whole novel with the help of a clone which is a product similar to a human being. According to Oxford Dictionary, a clone is a plant or an animal that is produced naturally or artificially from the cells of another plant or animal and is therefore exactly the same (biological features are the same) as it. The author says that five clones are given shape at the same time for different purposes. The author's concentration is on the clone named Inee among them. While the clone is travelling from one place to another place it happens to see a few people who are on different works for their livelihood and children for their amusement. Those men, women and children are called humanoids by the clone as they have not yet reached the physical or mental stage in evolution to identify them as humans. The Clone is in the future time and it sees the prehistoric stage people who had lived on distant Mother Earth.

In Daya Dissanayake's novel *The Clone,* the Clone is given shape to perform the task of monitoring all water resources in the world for any contamination and for any unusual changes in the flow (The Clone, 12). This clone maintains the 'ecological wisdom' as it has been acquiring knowledge since the 1348th Century and these clones have long life so the knowledge once acquired by them will not be destroyed. The below described context is apt in the part of this clone. In *Wisdom Sits in Places: Landscape and Language among the Western Apache* book, Keith H. Basso asks a question to his Apache informant, Nidee Elder Dudley Patteron who answers,

> Wisdom sits in places. It's like water that never dries up. You need to drink water to stay alive, don't you? Well, you also need to drink from places. You must remember everything about them. You must learn their names. You must remember what happened to them long ago. You must think about it and keep on thinking about it. Then your mind will become smoother and smoother. Then you will see danger before it happens. You will walk a long way and live a long time. You will be wise (Basso, 1996, 127).

In this novel *The Clone*, five clones, look alike, were given shapes to carry out different tasks. One of the clones Inee is narrating the whole novel. The author has compared the clones to the trees which are growing naturally not cloned trees. Like trees clones also do not grow old and die and hardly people will notice the growth of the trees and its changes. These clones are companionless and have no gender at all. There are no interactions with the other living creatures, no excretion, digestion and so on. All the clones have had an opportunity to develop a special skill, so the clone in this novel has opted to learn reading and writing of both major ancient languages and the current universal language. This clone Inee has a fancy of reading the books by laying its hands on a real printed book and by holding it up and trying to read it page by page turning the leaves. Actually, clones do not read stories or poems as they have no imaginations and they are asexual and live in isolation. But this clone in the novels is specially designed to read and develop its skill. Other clones "were engaged in similar assignments, controlling temperature, humidity, radiation and other such parameters, while many others were engaged in monitoring other life forms in our world. More senior clones were assigned the study of their neighbouring planets and our galaxy, to keep an eye on any changes or developments that could affect the planet" (*The Clone*, 14).

Reverence to Nature

Culture is observed significantly in the society which has a unique way of life. It reflects different modes of thoughts, actions and sensations of a social group. Culture comes out of the womb of a society but it is nurtured by the phenomena of nature. Basically, culture originates a social order and strategies within the limitations of their ecological structures. So, human beings and their community cannot escape from the influence of the environment and its influence on their behaviour. Man excels in his life with the advancements of his culture was a step away from nature as man has not yet identified the perfect definition of culture. In the present book *The Clone*, the culture, with time and space which are the part and parcel of human behavior, is portrayed very clearly. Over a period of time, the behavior of the people changed and developed a different kind of behavior. Daya Dissanayake writes about culture in one of his blog articles "Culture and Nature"

> When man enjoyed fresh fruits and leaves from the plant life around him he was living with nature. He departed from nature when he began to roast, burn and later boil his food. When man enjoyed the beauty of his surroundings he was with nature. When he began to alter his surroundings as his aesthetic senses 'developed' he began to interfere with nature. When he enjoyed the music of nature he belonged to nature. With his departure from nature, when he no longer could enjoy the music of nature, he had to create his own music. It was the same with art, though at first he is supposed to have used it as Homo sybolicus.

Vehement love and concern towards nature are significant to obtain ecological wisdom (Xu J Nangong, 2012). The way that humans worship nature varies across culture and religions. Buddhist monks preach that every living organism has the potential to become a Buddha. If one can give respect to nature he/she can obtain wisdom and can enjoy life. Human beings are responsible for what they do, vice versa, what they cannot do. Reverence for nature is identified in the novel *The Clone*.

Reverence for nature develops the inherent interconnectedness of all things in the world and it develops a sense of belonging and the emotional bonding to the earth. Three important things are observed in the novel, *The Clone* regarding this reverence for nature. Firstly, knowing and connecting one's true self, secondly, concerning and connecting both ecologically and spiritually the Mother Earth and maintaining with the human community.

Man is a social animal as he lives in groups from ancient to modern days. Thought of the nuclear family, prioritising 'his' own self, leaving customs and traditions, and so on come into the mind of the modern man. Like Daya Dissanayake's description of a person named Em Dee in the novel, man is not able to accept the presence of another man so he wants to be isolated and wants to rely on technology in the form of robots to do the household works. The author is frightened and assumes that,

> Even I was beginning to get the feeling that man had always been the biggest threat to the environment in which he lived. It appeared to me that every step he had taken with his new discoveries and inventions he had caused irreversible, irreparable destruction of natural resources. Homo sapiens had become, not only his own greatest enemy but the enemy of the entire Mother Earth (C, 25).

The author, Daya Dissanayake reminds the Gaia Hypothesis and says in this novel that the Earth is a self-regulating environment, a single living system and a kind of superorganism. Gaia, Mother Earth or the Universe suspects the danger that human beings started disturbing. As our ancestors said worshipping nature would be the best solution or ecological wisdom. The author writes in the article "Nature worship for world peace and harmony," all the human beings on the Earth worship the sky, the sun, the moon and the stars, rain and the rivers, the trees and the mountains as all nature belongs to humans and humans belong to nature.

Maintaining ecological wisdom is not difficult for a human being also but following the ethics of the culture they live in. Like this clone, another unique role is played by Mother Earth as an ecological worldview understands that the "flourishing of both human and non-human life" has "intrinsic value" and non-human life forms have value "independent of the usefulness these may have for narrow human purposes" (Naess and Rothenberg, 1989, 29). Undeniably, an ecological wisdom is often characterised by a large, more comprehensive, sense of life itself and may even consider Mother Earth itself to be alive or in some way similar to a living organism like the clone.

Holism

It is the concept that all the properties of a given ecosystem (physical, mental, and so on) cannot be determined or elucidated by its components alone. Instead, the system as a whole determines in a significant way how the components behave. Aristotle said that holism in Metaphysics "The whole is more than the sum of its parts." The harmonious relationships among the components or human beings and processes of social-ecological systems are reflected in any religious philosophy of holism, based on the recognition and understanding of the harmonisation between structure and function of a system between human and nature (Yan et al. 1993).

An ecosystem is combination of community and the environment. As the author says in the novel, without complete ecosystem there is no survival for any living being. He has given an example in the novel about mono-cultural plantation that is timber plants for paper making. He continued that by one plantation, there will be no possibility of balancing the complete ecosystem of many species of trees, shrubs, creepers, animals, birds and so on (C 52).

In this novel, the ecosystem of the human being is different from the ecosystem of the clone. Human beings have an open ecosystem whereas clones have a closed and controlled environment. Clones' kidneys, liver, pancreas are almost vestigial. Sickness, old age and death are all unknown to these clones.

Daya Dissanayake quoted Dr. James Lovelock's *A New Look at Life on Earth,*

> The entire range of living matter on Earth from whales to viruses and from oaks to algae could be regarded as constitution a single living entity capable of maintain the Earth's atmosphere to suit its overall needs and

> endowed with faculties and powers far beyond those of its constituent parts...[Gaia can be defined] as a complex entity involving the Earth's biosphere, atmosphere, oceans, and soil; the totality constituting feedback of cybernetic systems which seeks an optimal physical and chemical environment for life on this planet (C, 6-7).

An ecosystem is a combination of community and the environment. As the author says in the novel, without a complete ecosystem there is no survival for any living being. He has given an example in the novel about mono-cultural plantation that is timber plants for paper making. He continued that by one plantation, there will be no possibility of balancing the complete ecosystem of many species of trees, shrubs, creepers, animals, birds and so on(C, 52). Pollution has gone totally out of control due to the storage of water and food. The author has said about nuclear weapons, biological weapons, toxic pollution and even genetic pollution (C, 33). He said that Mother earth could not tolerate the arrogant humans destroying everything including self-destruction.

The clone explains the beauty of nature and how people spend their life by enjoying at the pool with the splashing of water. The true pleasure of nature is shown at every step in the novel by the author and how it was contaminated in various ways. The duty of the clone is to monitor the water resources in this novel. This clone is the witness for various human civilisations and how people become greedy by polluting the environment. Growing technology is another disastrous thing to the planet. At this juncture, the author has provided lot of examples in this novel, as the clone started recollecting that the technology used in the eras of Dwapara and Tretaa. Nothing had happened to them due to the usage of technology because they used that with ecological balance.

People think that due to the dependence on technology and machines, humanity will be annihilated. But the author says that technology is not a new term to 'invent' it is just 'rediscovery' which was existed if the Ramayana and the Mahabharata were taken into consideration to know about technology. For example, firstly, the birth of Lord Ganesha who was born of the bodily dust of Mother Parvathi, secondly, the birth of Draupadi and Drishtadyumna through yajna, thirdly, the birth of Sri Rama and his three brothers – with milk obtained from Yajna. Those were all possible only with the transference of an embryo from the womb of one mother to some other. The same is observed in the 20th century when the "Test Tube

Babies and Surogasea" came into existence. Another example for this is, in the Mahabharata i.e. Kauravas emerged from the womb of Gandhari in the form of a single egg and broken into hundred pieces. The embryo had grown in a pitcher. A few more examples were from Ramanyana i.e. Pushpaka Vimana which was used for ariel surveys by Ravana and in Agasthya Samhita, the manufacture of the electrical battery was described, using a copper plate, mercury amalgamated zinc plate, copper sulphate and moist saw-dust in an earthenware vessel. It is generated electricity releasing oxygen and hydrogen.

Nature evolved as a really well-balanced ecosystem that was always in equilibrium. Various cycles are observed in nature such as seasons, food, and so on. The human body is also like nature as it also follows different cycles. The tree is the place of enlightenment according to Buddha. The evolution of mankind had taken several million years but the collapse took only a few years and ultimate destruction may take place only in a few seconds. In history, there were strong shreds of evidence of great civilisations which destructed to its roots. The concerns of ecosystem and eco-criticism come into existence due to the arrogance of all human beings. Maintaining harmonious relationships in society, nature and in aspects are good for all human beings to survive on this planet. So, ecological wisdom is given utmost priority.

Conclusion

In this research paper, ecological wisdom is focused on with reference to Daya Dissanayake's *The Clone*. This study begins with a conceptual clarification so as to correctly define the focus and state the purpose of this research which is to read Daya Dissanayake's novel, *The Clone*, in the light of ecological wisdom. Secondly, principles of ecological wisdom and thirdly, scope and research perspectives on ecological wisdom are discussed. There is a wide scope for further research in this area as there are a number of principles are discussed under ecological wisdom by the great environmental writers. The present research is limited to only two principles such as reverence to nature and holism. Furthermore, only one novel of Daya Dissanayake, who is a great lover of deep ecology, is taken into consideration out of his nine novels. So, the researchers can focus their research on the other principles and novels of the same author. The researchers may choose many other writers of various periods to identify the perspectives of ecological wisdom and how it is identified in their novels. An extension of the analysis on literary devices will also provide a more comprehensive study. Thus, there lies a tremendous scope for research once evocative research like this is completed. Such research requires choosing one or two literary devices that are recommended in the particular area of research.

Works Cited

Basso, Keith H. 1996. *Wisdom Sits in Places: Landscape and Language among the Western Apache.* University of New Mexico Press,

Buell, Lawrence. 2001. *Writing for an Endangered World: Literature, Culture, and Environment in the U.S. and Beyond.* London: Belknap Press.

Dissanayake, Dayananda. 2012. *The Clone.* Serenity Publishers (Pvt) Ltd, Delhi. Print.

.... 2011. "Culture and Nature." *Blog Article.* Retrieved, 30 October 2021. http://www.saadhu.com/blog/2011/07/culture-vs-nature/

.... 2019. Extract from a plenary paper presented at the International Conference on "Environment, Culture and the Anthropocene," December 1 and 2, 2019 Berhampur University, Odisha.

.... 2019. Extract from a plenary paper presented at the International Conference on "Nature worship for world peace and harmony," December 1 and 2, 2019 Berhampur University, Odisha.

Garrard, Greg. *Ecocriticism.* 2004. Oxfordshire: Routledge.

Ghosh, Aitav. 2004. *The Hungry Tide*, New Delhi: HarperCollins.

Huggan, Graham and Helen Tiffin. 2010. *Postcolonial Ecocriticism: Literature, Animals, Environment.* Oxon: Routledge.

Lakshmi, Vijaya. 2018. 'Animal Symbolism in Paulo Coelho's Novels – A Select Study'. *International Journal of Innovative Research & Studies.* 8:2, 306-313.

.... 2018. "Fantastic Elements in Paulo Coelho's Novels – A Select Study." *English Language, Literature and Skills.* 7:1, 139-144.

.... 2021. "Pagan Symbolism in Paulo Coelho's *Brida*". *A Plethora of Thoughts*, Authors Press, New Delhi. p. 11-20

Næss, A. (1989). *Ecology, community and lifestyle: Outline of an ecosophy.* Cambridge: Cambridge University Press.

.... 1985a. *The World of Concrete Contents*, Inquiry 28, 417-428.

.... 1986a. "Intrinsic Value: Will the Defenders of Nature Please Rise," in M. E. Soulé (ed.), *Conservation Biology*, Sunderland: Sinauer 1986, pp. 504-515.

.... 1986b. "Self-realisation. An Ecological Approach to Being in the World," *Keith Memorial Lecture*, Murdoch University.

.... 1986. "The Deep Ecological Movement: Some Philosophical Aspects," *Philosophical Inquiry*, 8, pp. 1-31.

Schwartz B. Sharpe K. 2010. *Practical wisdom: the right way to do the right thing.* Riverhead Books, New York.

The Variety of Integral Ecologies Nature, Culture, and Knowledge in the PlanetaryEra. 2017. Eds. Adam Robbert, Sam Mickey, Sean Kelly. State University of New York Press, New York.

Xiang, W N. 2014. *Ecological wisdom for urban sustainability.* Landscape Urban Plan 121: 65-69.

Xu J, Nangong, M. & Longfellow, HW. 2012. "A Poetical-dwelling poet of ecological wisdom from the perspective of eco-criticism." *English Language Teaching* 5 (5): 85-100.

Yan J, Zhang Y & Wu X. 1993. "Advances of ecological engineering in China." *Ecological Engineering.* 2 (3): 193-215.

Yang, B. et al. 2019. "Where Does Ecological Wisdom Come from? Historical and Contemporary Perspectives: Innovative Approaches to Socio-Ecological Sustainability." p. 37-39. Retrieved 30 October 2021. https://www.researchgate.net/publication/330414947_Where_Does_Ecological_Wisdom_Come_from_Historical_and_Contemporary_Perspectives_Innovative_Approaches_to_Socio-Ecological_Sustainability

CHAPTER 9

A Critical Study on Significance of the Title *Thirst*

G. Srilatha

Daya Dissanayake, born on 8th March, 1947, is a Srilankan poet and a novelist. He is the first author of the first e-novel in Asia. He is the only Sri Lankan writer to receive the Sri Lankan State Literary Award for the best English novel three times. He also received SAARC Literary Award in 2013. His literary careers started in school where he contributed to the school magazine and wrote many short stories. Later he showed interest in subjects such as non-violence, history, archeology, Buddhism and religion. He portrays the rural underclass, monks, and money makers in his writings.

The novel 'Thirst' portrays the atrocious actions of the King. Throughout the novel the greediness of the King is evident. The King also exhibits pride and is adamant in each of his decisions. Due to such decisions the entire ecosystem is affected and disturbed. The novel opens with the Kings victory over conquering various territories. He immediately dreams of constructing a new palace. Then he goes ahead to construct a big dam. Every act of the King is associated with his self-glorification.

Coronation of the King

The King wanted the coronation to be the festivals of all festivals. He wanted it to be a memorable occasion and did not worry about the expenses. The people of the country were made to stand in the broad sunlight carrying the flags with the royal emblem and waving the flags. The gruesome act of the king is shown in the following lines,

> The King had returned to his city in triumph, after a long and hard fought war. He had marched on through towns and villages, rejoicing in his triumphs. Behind him he had left many thousands dead, many thousands more maimed for life. There were only widows and orphans and total

> devastation in the land he had passed through. Immediately after each battle, crows and rats and other scavenging animals had a feast on the bodies impaled on stakes by the roads leading to the villages. No one dared to bring down the bodies for a decent burial. The women could not help seeing the bodies of their sons and husbands and brothers, as they returned to what was left of their villages and farms. Younger mothers tried to keep their little children from seeing the gruesome scene of tortured bodies of their fathers (16).

Apart from men, elephants were also made a part of the celebration. Nearly one hundred and twenty elephants were decorated and led the parade. The elephants were brought from the nearby temples. The elephants suffered a long journey without proper rest and food. The mahouts were helpless. Though they knew that the elephants need rest, they were at the command of the King and had to obey them. Similarly, all the people were made to stand in the hot sun carrying the royal emblem. The King wanted it to be a memorable occasion. He enjoyed the procession and the grandeur.

The King appeared magnificent,

> The Mightiest of All Men, the Excellent Ruler of the universe, who had reduced all hostility to nothing, who had won lustrous glory, ascended the golden baldachin resting on the backs of two elephants is also covered in golden cloth. On His Majesty's head was a diadem sparkling as if it was another sun competing with the brilliance of the mid-morning sun (16).

The joy of conquest and celebration lasted for a short time and soon the King became restless. He had a desire to construct a big palace. The King feels that the palace is too small. He orders to the Chief Minister to find out a right place for the construction of the new palace. After a survey the King decides to select the construction site where the new palace would be constructed.

The choice of place where the palace would be constructed has shocked everyone. The King's grandfather has spent nearly twenty years to construct the garden. Over the years the garden has become a home for various birds and animals. The trees have grown huge in size. The destruction of the forest will be a heavy damage to the entire ecosystem. But the King fails to foresee the damage that would occur to nature which in fact affects the human life.

Construction of new Palace

The King's decision to construct a Palace at the cost of demolishing the garden is atrocious and foolish. While the King remains adamant in his choice the architect could visualises how beautifully the place has grown over the years,

> Around him, he saw, campaka, asoka, sal, patali, kadamba, malati and mango trees, Bees and butterflies hovered around the flowers. Squirrels and birds pecked at the sweet fruits. Peacocks strutted around ignoring or showing off to the wretched humans who were invading their privacy. There were several ponds, glowing in the sun light with their red and blue lotus flowers. The swans floated around lazily (19).

As the trees were plenty in the garden, the King orders to chop them and use for construction. The King was never happy with the plan of the architect. Every time the plan changed and there were fresh drawings. Whenever the change was made the building was more elaborate and more expensive to build. The architect proposed the plan to be constructed in eighteen months. But the King insisted it to be completed in three months which would cost three times more. More people should be employed and at the same time the quality of work should also be maintained.

The King would always make some suggestions for alterations on his visit to the construction site. The Chief Minister would not dare to say anything with the fear that he would be killed. Thus the ecosystem was disturbed and later destroyed. The peacefulness of the forest was erupted by chopping off the trees that were grown tall.

Even the queen on her visit would demand changes, especially on the interior décor and in the garden. "Colours on the walls had to be changed over and over as would the curtains and the furniture. Outside, where a pond had been built, she would have it filled again to make it a terrace. A path would be changed; plants would be uprooted and replanted, or discarded."

The architect was given only three months to complete the project. If the project is not completed in three months he could end up dead. He had no hope on the new palace. It may not last long. Roofs and the drains were of poor quality. Roofs and gutters could collapse, drains would get blocked. In some places he did not have enough space to lay down storm water drainage systems to his satisfaction, so the building could endure heavy monsoon rains.

> The first rains would create havoc with the roofs, and the drains. Roofs and gutters could collapse, drains would get blocked. In some places he did not have enough space to lay down storm water drainage systems to his satisfaction, so the building could endure heavy monsoon rains. There would also be problems with the sewage disposal. The locations of the bathrooms and toilets had been changed so many times, and there were

> too many pipes, with too many bends on them. They could get clogged up at any moment. The changing seasons and temperatures could also cause problems with the doors and windows, because some of the timber had not been properly seasoned (22).

Towards the deadline of completing the palace, more men had to work day and night. The accidents were also increased. The workers lost their hand, finger or even a leg. At last when the construction of the Palace came to an end the King invited monks to perform the rites.

Thus on the auspicious day monks chanted nonstop for seven days and seven nights. On the seventh day the king invited fifteen thousand monks. The King also wanted to offer food for all who had worked, but as they were nearly two hundred and fifty thousand, the ministers suggested that it would be difficult to cook large quantity of food. Hence dry ration was distributed to them.

The greediness of the King is depicted again and again in the novel. The King's happiness in the new palace lasted only for a short period. He soon invited all the ministers and announced that he had a big dream to construct a large dam.

Construction of Dam

The King was happy in the new palace for only a short time. He soon desires to,

> I have to carve my name in gold, in the history of our country. Even to the end of time, my name should be preserved…… I am going to build the largest tank in the country. I am going to give my name, so people will talk about me forever, and be grateful to me. They will build temples in my name. My statue will be placed inside these temples. People will offer flowers and incense and light lamps at my feet. I will be worshiped as a god, after my death (25).

Thus the King's thirst for power and greediness is evident. Initially the King wanted to conquer the country, later construct a palace and now a dam. The chief minister insists that there are many dams and now it is not necessary. Reta discussed with the Chief Irrigation Engineer, Hagara. They had drawn many proposals.

According to the King the new project could bring wealth and prosperity to the country and to the people of the region. Though the project may lead to the destruction of a very old temple the King assures to build new temple in a different place. The King wants to construct a big dam and also he wants to ingrain his name on the stone. The Biggest dam would also cost enormous but he is adamant to listen. He overweighs the benefits of the dam, but ironically it results in the destruction of the nature and man.

The monks were not interested in relocation. The King refuses to show mercy towards his people. He was determined on constructing the dam. The Chief Minister fears of losing his life and lacks confidence to speak to the King on the drawbacks of the dam. His daughter Puna volunteer's to support her father.

Tisaguta thera tried to stop the construction of the dam. He elaborated to the people on the harm that the project could do.

> These trees are a national treasure. The forest has been here millions of years and should be saved. We have to save them for the sake of our children, and their children. No one has the right to destroy anything that is gifted to us by nature. When the forest is destroyed, it destroys the food and shelter not only for us but also for so many creatures. The king can provide land for you, but who will provide food and shelter for the innocent birds and the animals (49)?

He also warns them that the land that is offered to them is not so fertile. There are too many rocks and the soil is not so good for cultivation. The people were not ready to understand the situation. Finally, Tisaguta thera sat under a tree as a protest.

The workers did not move him as he is a Buddhist monk and he should be treated with respect. Taba, the Project Manager of the construction of the dam had to ensure the work is completed on time. The monk was from the nearby village and all respected him. Taba was helpless in moving the monk from that site. Uti, the engineer pounces on Taba for the delay. Taba pleads the monks to leave the place as they have to execute the orders given by the King. Taba meets the chief minister to inform about the situation. The chief Minister informed the King. The King immediately orders that the project should not be delayed for any reason. The King assures his authority to deal with any problem and not waste time in the project.

While all the work men remained in silent Taba requests the monk to give away his protest. The time allotted to the chief minister is very less. If his orders are not implemented the next thing is the person would be put to death. In order to complete the task more and more people were employed from far and near. The King admired his name, fame and glory. The people relentlessly struggled to execute the King's order.

Taba tells the engineer that the monk is determined to protest against the construction of the dam. Uti says, "We cannot stop work now. We have already completed more than three fourths of the work. The King will never agree?

> We have to inform His Majesty
>
> He will cut your head off, if you tell him that we have to abandon the work. Why can't we just pull this old man out of here?"
>
> The villagers respected the monk. They treat him as they treat the King.
>
> The monks rejected the construction of dam. The villagers valued the monks. The temple and the values that the Buddhist monks have generated are very fruitful (53).

Tisaguta thera remained in the same place, he neither accepted the food nor food offered to him. He appeared as a part of the stone pillar, a part of the dam under construction. The workers worked causing no noise so that the monk is not disturbed. They hold monk at a very high esteem. They do not dare to disturb him. The monk not even opened his eyes. Two days passed on and Taba thought the monk would give up when he cannot bare the hunger and thirst. Neither the monk would give up the fast nor would the villagers persuade him to give up.

The villagers respected the monk and they worked without making any noise as they valued the monk. Most of them are aware of Therta as he was one of the respected monks in the region. The King was heedless and deaf to the agitators. The King showed no mercy in fact he insists to continue the work as though the monk did not exist there. Uti orders to the workers to continue the work. The workers refuse as their priest is seated there yet they remained restless and helpless before the authority of the King.

> The engineer threatened the worker. He pulled out his sword and threatened the workers. Two men were injured and were dead. The soldiers were deputed to monitor the work. The boulders and rocks were pulled to the edge of the half completed dam. The monk did not move. All the workers were helpless. The dust rose like a curtain across the brutal scene. When the dust got settled they could not see the monk. Thus the falling boulders killed the monk (57).

Thus the work progressed leaving the rocks falling on the Monk so he was buried alive. The relentless work of the workers continued only to kill Tisaguta thera. Cita the young sister screamed at the engineer. She was determined to save the valley. The lives of the people are of no value to the King; even the monk's life is not spared.

Mahavapi

After the construction of the dam, it was a surprise for every one as there was less water in the new dam. The dam also appeared smaller than some of the tanks in the city. When Taba explain to the King, "This is all the water we can collect from the river and the flow below the dam has completely dried up already" As a result there will be no water for the people who live downstream. The King was unhappy as he expected a greater flow of water. He asks the engineer if something could be done. The engineer suggested that they have to destroy the dam built further up so that can bring sufficient water to this reservoir.

Reta refers to that dam as a very old one which was constructed hundreds of years ago so that the water could be diverted to the main canal that leads to the tanks around the city. The King orders to immediately break that dam so that water will flow into this tank. Moreover, he wants this to be the biggest tank in the country. The King's order was taken up by Uti. He took more workmen to start working on demolishing the old dam. This action would cut off the water supply to the entire city. Uti seemed to be an expert at demolition as well as construction. He knew the exact points where the rocks should be loosened, where to start digging into the earthworks.

The breached dam did not show any change in the village or in the city tanks. It remained unnoticed by the city people for some time. Taba had to live with the guilt of completing the dam that would destroy a fertile, beautiful valley and disrupt the lives of hundreds of families.

The water flowed from higher levels to lower levels and that is the plan of nature. But the foolishness of the King causes a great damage to the environment. The water from the new dam would drown most of the villages. Cita considers her duty to alert all and make them understand that sooner everyone would be ruined. Tisaguta thera could not do anything to save the village. His sister Cita also fails to do anything to protect the people. The villagers are aware that their days are numbered. The water swelled and it was a threat to all in the village. The people slowly packed their things and moved away. The villagers were given new land where they can construct new house. Cita wanted to plant a Banyan tree or a Bodhi tree where her brother was buried. She refused to move to the new village like other people.

The people in the village were too busy serving the King and making Money. Cita determines to inform them on the great threat that is awaiting them. She ensures to protect them. The news of their threat spreads far and wide, people began to come in large numbers to know their plight. Cita addresses the large gathering and said the Mahavapi project will soon destroy the village and the environment. The people realised that sooner or later there will be scarcity of water. The only solution is they should repair the dam. Among the crowd there was King's son. The Prince appeared bare bodied and stood near Cita and spoke to the people.

The Prince gives a picture of the threat of the city and how they would struggle without water. Children would cry for water, women would not have water to wash vessel, animals would cry for water. The Prince alerts the crowd that they should identify the cause of the suffering and remove that cause. According to the Prince it is time to put an end to King's destruction. He says by simply sitting in temples, praying and meditation our suffering will not come to an end. They should eliminate the root cause. As the root cause of the suffering is the King they should destroy the King. All the villagers marched towards the palace to attack the King.

> The men broke into the palace buildings. They lost all further interest in the uprising and the issue of water. Some began looting, carrying away any valuable items they could get hold of. Others went in search of the young female servants. Cita watched from a distance as the kitten she had nurtured turned into a vicious tiger.
>
> The king had been dragged out of the building. Someone had thrown a rope around his neck and was dragging the king along the ground.
>
> 'Let's hang him from the nearest tree' one of the ministers, who had crossed over to the prince shouted (67).

The Prince claims that he wanted a healthy nation to rule over. His statistics say that the King has murdered 6,425 women and children. The Prince had travelled to many villages and collected the right information. The King had committed a crime. He had killed a Buddhist monk. Nearly one million men, women and children had to die of thirst. The Prince says it is the time to act. He says Destiny is in our hands. The Prince leads the crowd towards the palace.

> The King had committed serious crimes. Killing Tisaguta thera was the worst deed the king had committed. May be he deserved punishment, but did they have to murder him the way they did. Did one crime justify another? All she had wanted was to save their village, their forests and the fields and the birds and animals in their valley. She did not want to see any one die because of it. No one had the right to take another's life. Life was sacred, whether it was that of a Buddhist monk or a king or a simple peasant, or even a predatory bird soaring high up in the sky looking for its prey (70).

Every act of the King finally led to deforestation, demolishing the ancient temple, disturbing the ecosystem, and destroying the garden. The greediness of the King to lead a luxurious life and achieve name and fame has been at the cost of many lives. Trees are a great source of life but by cutting the trees and demolishing the garden the entire ecosystem is disturbed. While the Architect estimates that it would take nearly eighteen months to complete the project, the King wanted it in three months. The dam becomes a threat to all the villagers. Thus the unquenchable thirst of the King for name and fame leads to destruction of the ecosystem and the lives of the people.

Works Cited

Dissanayake, Daya. *Thirst.* Peliyagoda, Sri Lanka, ISBN 955-06508-5-8 2004.

CHAPTER 10

Filial Affection in Daya Dissanayake's *Miracle under the Kumbak Tree*

Palakurthy Dinakar

Daya Dissanayake is a celebrated bi-lingual author who writes in English and Sinhala. He was born, brought up and lives in Sri Lanka. He was a student of History and Religion. He received Sri Lankan State Literary Award thrice in 1998, 2007 and 2013 for his English novels *Kat Bitha* (his debut novel), *Eavesdropper* and *Miracle under the Kumbuk Tree* respectively. *The Saadhu Testament* is the first ever electronic novel by an Asian Author is produced by Daya Dissanayake. He also published the first e-novel in Sinhala language entitled, *Wessan Novu Wedun.* He shared the Swarna Pusthaka Award for the Best Sinhala novel in 2007 for *Chadraratnage Bhavantara Charikava.* The present novel *Miracle under the Kumbuk Tree* expresses the filial love of a daughter to her father. This is the story of Babli, a very methodical girl, the only daughter of Edward Silva and Jasintha Samaranayake, daily paid workers on the coconut estates around their remote village Mahakele about 5 km from Anamaduwa in Sri Lanka.

Babli loves her parents like many other children in the world but her love is very significant that she wanted to sacrifice her life to give a new lease of life to her father. Her father was suffering from a disease called Cardiomayopathy, a heart disease in the advanced stage which he was a pathetic bootlegger. The only way is to save his life to go for heart transplantation. Timothy Foundation, an NGO agreed to finance the surgery, if they could find a suitable heart, usually from a victim of an accident. When Mr. Brendon Crain, representative from Timothy Foundation had said it to Babli, she decided to arrange a heart to her father by any means. As she could not get a heart for transplantation, she decided to give her own heart. So she swallowed a large number of sleeping pills and she wished that her heart could be transplanted to her father as a last resort. She forwarded an email to Mr. Brendon which sounded very serious. Babli in her email said 'she had decided to take her own life, so her heart could be taken to be transplanted in her father, who is dying from a serious heart condition. (5) She informed the foundation the address of her body and the telephone number for immediate assistance to get her heart out in her email. Babli knew the email address and other details of the foundation as she had good acquaintances with the foundation because she was educated from their financial assistance. Babli also posted on her Twitter page, 'Going to kill myself tonight, so my father could live on with my heart.' She was of the opinion that the Foundation would make all the arrangements for the surgery and father would be rescued from the danger. She also had an opinion that no one would tell her father about her sacrifice till he had recovered from the danger.

But much against to her expectations, Babli was rescued by the company colleagues and she was shifted immediately to the hospital by the CEO Mr. Damien Selveratnam who helped her in getting proper medical help. She was ashamed of her ignorance regarding heart transplantation after her recovery from the suicide attempt. She was also ashamed of not thinking about her parent's lives without her support. When Babli was out of danger, Damien wanted to take her to a neurologist to cure her 'Asperger's Syndrome (Pervasive Development Disorder), which could send her to a depression leading to suicide. Some her colleagues have the opinion that she might have taken that decision because,

> Her helplessness in trying to save his father's life that sent her in to a depression. I can't believe that a sensible girl like this could make such a foolish attempt. If her body had not been discovered for some time, then her sacrifice could have been in vain, even if our doctors could do a transplant. I doubt if we have the facilities in our hospitals. Then there is the legal issue, would the police release the body of a suicide victim without a post mortem. (9)

Babli's father Edward Silva @ Eddie is a miserable drunkard. He works in the day and drinks by evening. He drinks without a limit and when he drinks he loses his control and consciousness. He batters his wife and daughter scolds them with filthy language without any reason. Even the neighbours and the villagers were all vexed with the boorish behavior of Eddie. Babli's childhood was gripped in fearfulness and tension and she was never dared to see the face of her father because of his arrogant behaviour. Her father would always shout, scold and even thrash her. When Eddie enters the house during the late hours of the night, he would keep shouting at her mother and she retaliates in the same pace. As a result he beats both the mother and the daughter. When Babli cries Eddie would say, 'You have been crying for no reason, so now you have a reason to cry. He would beat her the way the cart driver beats the bull, or their neighbour beats their dog when it begins to howl at night.' (11) Babli didn't know what hunger was as she had been in the state of hungry all the time thinking that it was a natural burning sensation in the stomach to everyone. Babli recollects her childhood experiences, 'Once when father threw his roti into the garden saying only dogs can eat such food, Babli had run out and picked it up. She was so hungry that she wiped the dust and dirt off it and took a bite… 'Who told you to pick it up?' her father growled at her. 'I threw it for the dogs and only dogs can have it.'(12)

Once Babli was seriously wounded with burns in an accident in which she had tripped over the rickety table leg and fallen, with the bottle lamp that was on the edge of the table toppling over her spilling the kerosene oil on her. This incident turned to be a good opportunity for Babli because she got the opportunity to meet the NGO 'Timothy Foundation, which provided her nourishing food and medicine. They also built a house for her family and sponsored her schooling. Babli had not bothered about his father's reaction about the sacrifice she had made to save her father's life. She never thought of the idea that he had lost a daughter to gain a second lease of life. But her plan was failed and she was saved. She was in despair and frustration and tried to push back her tears. She did not open her mouth for any question posed at her because if she started answering the questions, she would be bombarded with many more questions by her colleagues in the office and others also. She decided to explore all available avenues and possible ways and means to save her father from that dreadful heart disease. Babli prayed all Gods of all religions and visited temples and churches in equal number. The people of her village saw her only inside the places of worship most of the times. 'They were amazed as they have not seen any one who visited both the temple and the church. The Buddhists could see her offering flowers at the Bo Tree and the Stupa and the shrine room, whispering her gatha with her hands together on her head. The Christians could see her at the mass, kneeling at the pew, singing hymns, kneeling before the priest to receive the mass.' (17)

When Babli recovered from her illness, she expected some sympathetic words from her father like, 'I didn't save your life when you were a child so you could throw it away on a person who did not deserve such sacrifice ... If you love me then you should be with me till I die. You can't leave me alone ...What use would your heart be to me, if you were not here with me.' (20) But Eddie never uttered even a word like 'thanks' to Babli. Very soon she realised that it's her foolishness to expect such expressions that she knew from her childhood. He was a father only by name and she didn't feel that he is not even a fatherly figure. Eddie used to say to his wife and daughter in intoxication condition, 'The two of you will be the death of me.' The words had begun to haunt her ever since her father fell ill. Similarly he had used many harsh words in his anger, but these words seemed to be a premonition, when she thought about them now. Babli felt that her father might use all these words that he was not getting enough money from his wife for drinking and moreover he wanted to have a son instead of a daughter. Babli didn't want to be 'the death of her father'; instead she wanted to save him from death. She was waiting for a suitable opportunity but she never imagined that her death would fetch misery to the family. Her parents may not be in a position to survive without Babli's financial assistance eventhough Eddie has got a new lease of life. 'That's what I mean. Even if her father got a new heart and a new lease of life, how could he survive without any income? His life would have been worse off than if he had died of heart failure, because even the support they got from their daughter would have been lost.' (23)

The village elders and spiritual heads like Chief Monk, Priests and Missionary people decided to help Eddie to get out of his habit of drinking and they were also ready to help him recover from his heart disease. These two problems are intertwined. Eddie always says 'he drinks to forget his illness, his impending death, the pain. He can also ask why he should not enjoy the few days left for him to live.' (23) Eddie was only 50 years old but looks older than his age and he depends on his daughter's earnings. The Chief Monk advised the other religious people to train Eddie to practice 'anapanasati bhavana' which could help him a lot for his speedy recovery from ill health. 'It is the first subject of meditation in the Mahasatipatthana Sutta. It is said that the Buddha had begun his meditation with Anapanasati on the night he attained Enlightenment.' (29) Further the Chief Monk advised, "for the time being, let him take his medicine. That will also give him more confidence … taking these drugs for a brief period could not do much harm. Recently a doctor who came to the temple told me that some of the doctors now believe that prayer and meditation also helps in healing, he said that they now realise there is a spiritual dimension to health, and also that most modern medicine did not have the same effect on all the patients who used them.' (39)

Babli had many bad experiences during her childhood. 'The smell of bootleg liquor had lingered with her throughout her childhood, and whenever she came home. It was always nauseating, stifling her breath, killing her appetite. The loss of appetite was the only blessing she could count on, because it made her forget her hunger pains.' (41) The same kind of foul smell comes from both her parents. Her father started drinking a long ago and her mother fought against this bad habit at the initial stage but over a period of time she was also habituated to it as Eddie's friend Jayaratne started selling 'moonshine', the bootleg alcohol in Eddie's house. Those drunken parents would never identify the hunger pangs of their child. The worst of all things was that they use raw filth to abuse one another which resulted in a scuffle usually.

Irrespective of her childhood experiences, Babli was so kind and positive in her attitude. She had to spend some days in the hospital due to the fire accident and her bad experiences at the hospital haunted her throughout her life. When she grew up and working in Colombo she used to go to the Children's Hospital once a month. She would help the sick and the needy in the hospital. She would give toys, eatables and other essential commodities to them. She looked for the abandoned child and would try to converse and extend her hand of cooperation in the form of medicines, clothes, soft toys and some eatables to the child. Babli was shocked to know that the sick children's mothers had to sell their bodies to get medicines and food for their children. 'She felt a great relief at the thought that her mother did not have to sacrifice her body to earn a little money and food to be with her daughter. Babli had seen the vultures, the pimps and the touts hanging around the children's hospital looking out for helpless young mothers.' (47) So Babli decided to donate her entire salary for the welfare of the poor children in order to save them and their mothers. But it became impossible for her, so she decided to donate major portion of her income to the welfare of the needy.

Babli was not sent to school by her parents. But when Timothy Foundation convinced them by giving new white frock, school bag and other essential things for her study they had to send her school. Babli's parents agreed to send her to the school because the foundation had threatened them that the police and the government will take stringent action if the child is not sent to the school. Babli was a meritorious student in her studies. When Babli got seven D's and the second best results in her class, she immediately rushed to her mother and declared the results. 'Hm', was the only response she got from her mother! Her mother did not realise the importance of the education and the result. Moreover Javi said. 'So what? can you get a job now?' (51) Babli was humiliated with this response from her mother. At the same time Babli's classmate who got the eight Ds celebrated her victory with her family. Babli felt that she had no one to share either the joy or the pain at the same time she had on one to share her victory and her defeat.

Babli was not happy with the brutal behavior of her father since her childhood. Sometimes she was so furious with her father for hitting her cruelly; sometimes she would imagine that he was not her real father. She imagines, 'Eddie had stolen her from a rich family. Her real family had gone on a pilgrimage and she had got lost and Eddie had found her… Her family had gone with her to see Wesak pandals and in the crowd; Eddie had grabbed her and run away…She was in a park with her real mother when for a moment her mother had been talking to another woman Eddie had come and snatched her… She was playing on the beach when a big wave had crashed into her and pulled her out into the sea. Eddie who had been on a fishing boat had seen her and pulled her aboard, but had decided not to inform her parents or the police, instead had run away to Anamaduwa with her. (52)

Babli would imagine that the police were looking for her and they would come to take her to her real parents. Then she would have a nice mansion, a big car, lovely parents and friends to play and relatives to share the pleasures and pains. Moreover the police would arrest Eddie and Javi for their crime. She would get chocolates, ice cream, new clothes and many toys. 'Her real father would carry her in her arms; she would go to sleep on his lap while he stroked her hair. Her real mother would feed her while she got dressed for school or in the evening when she was too sleepy to eat. She would have friends to play with like friends of her own age, and friends of other rich families. They would have rooms full of toys. Dolls, bicycles. Toy cars, airplanes and guns. Her imagination was also limited to things she knew about, thing she saw at the weekly market and with the families who came from the city.' (53) Babli really enjoyed such dreams particularly when she had received a beating from her father and scolding from her mother.

Babli was denied of some of the small pleasures. Her parents were not loving and caring. She had neither friends to play nor brothers or cousins to fight with. She had no relatives, kith or kin to exchange her feelings and accomplishments. Even when she goes to school the children did not play with her because of many reasons. Some of the students would say, 'We don't really mind playing with you, but mother said not to play with you', some children had told her. .. Yes, your father is a very bad person and we shouldn't talk to you … Your father sells kasippu … My sister says you must be drinking it too. (53)

Babli always compares her life with the life of other children in the village. Her suspicion continued about her parentage, when she saw the love the other children got from their parents and the hatred and insults she received. As she grew, this suspicion had increased when she did not find her birth certificate neither in the school nor at the house. 'This thought had haunted her on and off, that the birth certificate, her National Identity and her life itself as Babli Silva was a fraud, that she had committed an offence by having two birth registrations and thus two identities. This could also explain her father's reluctance to face the inquiry that was held in the city, before they issued her birth certificate. His reluctance and his nervousness had been interpreted as his natural backward attitude and illiteracy.'(54)

The Chief Monk explained to Babli and others that according to Lord Buddha, there are four kinds of people on this earth. 1) One who is not concerned of the well-being of oneself, nor of the others (like Eddie who neglected himself and his family). 2) One who is concerned of the wellbeing of others, but not of oneself (like Babli who was ready to sacrifice her heart to save her father). 3) One who is concerned of the well-being of oneself, but not of the others (like many people in the world). 4. One who is concerned of the well-being of oneself (*Attahita*) as well as the well-being of others (*Parahita*). The last one is considered to be the noblest of all. He also explained the extraordinary powers of Bodhi tree. Babli believed in supernatural powers of the Bodhi tree which had been worshipped in India for more than 5000 years. So she decided to offer Bodhi puja as a ritual for the sake of good-health of her father. She could not claim herself as Buddhist, but offering Bodhi puja as a helpless daughter to save her father.

> Babli walked by her father's side as he went up to the altar, wondering how she could get him to believe in the powers of this sacred tree, which had helped heal billions of humans through the ages. She wanted to tell him about all the miracles surrounding the Bo Tree she had heard about, but communication had always been a major problem between father and daughter. (68)

Babli would remain calm when her father was around during her childhood. With the passing of time, this fear is replaced by dislike and turned to hatred. She could not share her feeling with anyone in the world about her parents particularly about her father. Babli had a soft corner for her mother who did not leave her during her childhood like some other miserable mothers who went for foreign countries as maids. Babli could not recall a single instance when she had asked her father to stop drinking because she was very much afraid of him. Babli was determined to continue her further studies in disciplines like Law, Business Management through Open University but it couldn't be realised when her father fell ill. She had to go home more frequently; sometimes she had to skip lectures.

Babli used to take a little doll wherever she goes. She holds it to her chest when she goes to sleep. She keeps it with her on the table when she studies. She used to keep it in her school bag. When Babli was in hospital after the fire accident, her father gave it to her. It was the only link with her father. Thinking about the doll and the pathetic condition of her father Babli developed a sympathetic approach. She wanted to save her father from this life threatening disease. But her attempt of giving her heart to her father was failed so she wanted to help her father by performing religious rituals of both Buddhists and Christians. Babli approached Chief Monk for help, who said, 'Talk to him. Show him that you love him, give him a reason to live, convince him that you need him. He is not aware of half the things you are doing for him … It is to show how much you care for him. (95) Babli replied, 'I don't know what to call him. I have never called him *appachchi*, or *thaththa*, and he has never called me *duwa* or even Babli. The Chief Monk advised Babli that caring is more important than curing. He further advised her to spend more time at least during weekends which can improve the health of her father. He also suggested that it would do more good than all the pujas and other religious rituals. Babli made up her mind to talk to her father because she was determined to save her father's life. She had to talk to him, get close to him, and help him to regain his health. She wanted to break the ice. She wanted to face him 'face to face' and wanted to talk directly.

Babli's only dream is to help her father regain his health. On the contrary Eddie advised Babli not to waste her life and energy on him as he was on his death bed. But she was not in a position to listen to her father and very much determined to save his life. She said to her father 'You and amma are all I have. I can't live without you … Thaththa,' (98.) The word 'thaththa' came to her naturally and she had never called him thaththa till that day and she was worried it would sound strange on her tongue. By listening to such words Eddie burst into tears and both father and daughter hugged each other. Till now Eddie had touched his daughter only in anger, to hit her, to hurt her but for the first time he touched her with love and affection. With the passing of time Eddie is getting his strength back and his heart muscles grew stronger. He became healthy because of his daughter's care and concern; love and affection. Damien the CEO of Babli company said to Eddie, 'You must really be proud of her. You are so lucky to have a girl like this as your daughter' he said. He saw the gleam of tears on Babli's eyes. 'You won this battle against all odds. You are really great.' (113)

The novel ends when Brendon sent two sets of test reports of heart to a hospital in Germany for their medical opinion. The hospital authorities replied that the reports do not belong to the same patient. 'According to the earlier report, the patient would not have survived for so long without heart transplantation. The second report showed no record of any cardiac problems and no traces of any such history' (115). It was the result of the real love of a daughter for her father who saved him from the danger. It was proved once again that 'caring is very important than curing.'

Works Cited

Dissanayake, Daya. *Miracle under the Kumbak Tree.* Sarasavi. Colombo, 2012.

CHAPTER 11

"Poverty of Wealth" – A Study of Daya Dissanayake's *Moonstone*

S. Karthik Kumar

> There was a time when meadow, grove, and stream,
> The earth, and every common sight,
> To me did seem
> Apparelled in celestial light,
> The glory and the freshness of a dream.
> It is not now as it hath been of yore; –
> Turn wheresoever' I may,
> By night or day.
> The things which I have seen I now can see no more.
> ....
> Whither is fled the visionary gleam?
> Where is it now, the glory and the dream?
>
> (Wordsworth, "Intimations: Ode")

Culture plays a vital role in conditioning the mindset of the people. We are so much influenced by cultural forces that we use a good number of words without realising their significance. In today's context, the meanings of "modernity", "culture," and "civilisation" are simply taken for granted. They are generally used as allies of wealth, social status, access to information, etc. "Standard of Living", which is determined by one's wealth and social status has become more important than "Standard of Life", which is determined by values of life.

Human life is how one lives rather than what one lives. There was a time when life was simple but profound and intense; but now things have changed a lot and it has become busy, complicated but very shallow. People seem to be happy and successful outwardly but suffer from loneliness and alienation.

Humanity has steadily been weaned away from the traditional patterns of life that ensured the harmonious coexistence between the human civilisation and the Planet. The traditional way of life was not against "progress" and "growth" as it is commonly mistaken to be. But it insisted on and ensured the overall growth of human personality, both the external and the internal. It also implied that the individual growth was essentially collateral to the growth of humanity as one composite body. In fact, it kept reminding the fact that the humans were one among the many species on the planet and, thus, the harmony between the human and the nonhuman world was maintained. Simplicity paved way for peace and the sense of harmony resulted in contentment, and on the whole, life was meaningful.

All this changed with the advent of the modern civilisation. Modernity is associated with the rise of reason and intellectualism. Though it began in the west, it spread across the globe during the period of European colonisation. The rise of reason was a severe blow to the peaceful coexistence of humanity with the environment. With the sense of reason humans began to view to themselves as the centre of the universe and they came to believe the other species are simply for the benefit and pleasure of humanity. It resulted in the dangerous shift from eco-centrism to anthropocentrism.

With the advent of industrialisation there was a regular exodus of people from villages to industrial centres which later became towns and cities. The towns and cities have become centres of modern civilisation that represent the permanent divide between the rural and the urban, nature and culture, and tradition and modernity. Even as industrial civilisation had brought many comforts and eased life to a large extent, its nexus with capitalism and urbanisation brought about a lot of changes in human perception of life. Materialism crept in that endangered the value of mutual coexistence and harmony with the nonhuman world. The microchip revolution by the end of the twentieth century was yet another wave of civilisation that brought about a new age in the history of humans that permanently estranged the humans from the Planet. It is a paradox that the wonderful technology of communication has also contributed to the sense of alienation and isolation that mankind most suffers from today. Even as we celebrate that the globe has shrunk into a mere village, communication, both interpersonal and intrapersonal, has suffered its worst only during this phase of civilisation. The steady advancement of communication technology and the increased dependence on the electronic gadgets have made humans believe more in virtual reality rather than reality. The increasing exposure to and interaction with the artificial world has come in the way of humans communicating with themselves, other humans, and the planet. The postmodern man, in brief, is not only estranged from others, but also from himself. The incredible growth in science and technology has been responsible for the growth of wealth; but it has also resulted in severe loss of peace. However, it is to be clarified that the root cause of the problem lies not with technology itself but with the inability of humans to come to terms with the developments. The abundance of material comforts and wealth that surround modern life has rendered the humans oblivious of the need for a balanced spiritual growth. This was lamented by W. B. Yeats even as early as the 1920's:

> Turning and turning in the widening gyre
> The falcon cannot hear the falconer;
> Things fall apart; the centre cannot hold;
> Mere anarchy is loosed upon the world,
> The blood-dimmed tide is loosed, and everywhere
> The ceremony of innocence is drowned;
> The best lack all conviction, while the worst
> Are full of passionate intensity. ("The Second Coming")

The crisis the world faces today is more a spiritual crisis rather than a material one. The crisis has to be solved by artists and philosophers rather than by scientists. Technology can provide external comforts but it cannot solve the inner crisis. It is at this juncture creative writers and their writings assume important. They keep reminding humanity of the true purpose and meaning of life. Being visionaries, they are able to see through the present and foretell what is to come.

Moonstone by Daya Dissanayake is a seminal work of fiction that deals with the most serious crisis that humanity in general and the youth in particular are facing today – restlessness. The novel portrays the contemporary human predicament in such a graphic manner that it exposes the emptiness of "modern" life that seems to be very busy – "full of sound and fury but signifies nothing." The author himself has described his novel: "This is a work of fiction. The story was written on the basis that fiction is stranger than the truth." It is the story of Sandaruwan alias Chandraratne, a Sri Lankan-born technologist who is hailed as a Sri Lankan Bill Gates. He is the founder chairman of the leading IT Company, Thakshana.com, and one of the richest in the world. The novel opens when Chandraratne has become Sandaruwan, an established businessman who has his network of IT industry across the globe. He owns an island of his own "Supaditi" from where he can control his entire business. Only as the novel proceeds, we come to know about his early life in Sri Lanka.

In Sri Lanka, he was a poor rustic boy who had lost his mother at a very early age. He was brought up with motherly care by his father, Romiel, who was reserved, innocent rustic man. By sheer hard work accompanied by good luck, he could rise himself as a software engineer. He moved to the US where he emerged as a leading IT industrialist. Once he arrived in the US, he wanted to disconnect himself from his past life in Sri Lanka: "He was born again after reaching Los Angeles, when he changed his name to Sandaruwan. He had decided to change his name, soon as he learnt that he had won the Green Card. He decided to leave Chandraratne behind, in Sri Lanka, dead and buried, and forgotten" (*Moonstone*, 24).

Now Sandaruwan has everything. His island is self-sufficient. It is a mini paradise on earth from where he could monitor his thousands of employees spread across the world. He can do anything anywhere without moving out of his home in Subaditi. In spite of his material wealth, professional success and social accomplishment, he feels poor in his heart of hearts.

> Almost all of his staff, several thousands, scattered across the globe, were happy working for him and enjoyed their work. Yet all his success and recognition still did not make Sandaruwan happy. He had one worry nagging at his mind, all the time. His father was his problem. The only problem which could not yet be solved with all his knowledge, power and money. He could not enjoy all his achievements and lead a good life on his island while his fatherwas going through a miserable lonely life in the village in Sri Lanka. (*Moonstone*, 22)

Sandaruwan feels guilty of having neglected his father. Ever since he got his first employment in Sri Lanka, he has never met him. His father had done him everything when he was motherless boy. His father does not even know that it is his son who has become a world-famous multimillionaire. As long as he was busy in establishing his business, he was not bothered by the memory of his father. Accumulation of wealth and accomplishment of success kept him driving from behind. Once he has become an established industrialist, when he has time to read and think, he is reminded of his past, the life he spent with his father. He feels that he has done nothing to his father. He realises that he has failed to take care of his father. This makes him restless and he suffers from a guilt which no one other than himself knows.

Dissanayake titles one of the chapters in the novel as "Poverty of Wealth." Sandaruwan is poor for he has failed to show love to his father. He knows well that his father will not take it seriously. But the sense of guilt torments him like anything.

> Sandaruwan could not concentrate on his work. Sometimes, when he was deeply in thought, a blurred image of his father would appear on one of the monitors, as a reflection, covering whatever was on display.
>
> Father was squatting on the front porch, chewing beetle. Was he thinking of Chandraratne? Was he expecting his son to come home, to see him? Did he know that Chandraratne was dead and Sandaruwan was now settled down in the Seychelles?
>
> Father may not even know that Chandraratne had left his country of birth. Father would not know if he was dead or alive. Chandraratne was dead, for all practical purposes. He had a new life now. A re-birth or a re-incarnation. (*Moonstone*, 30)

Sandaruwan wanted to something to his father by way paying his debt of gratitude. At the same, he has hidden his identity from the public for a long time. He is apprehensive that his father will not come to live with him even if he makes an earnest appeal. So, he tries to solve the issue through technology with which he is well-versed.

Sandaruwan has a strong faith that he can get his father born to him in his father's next birth. If his father is born to him, he will have an opportunity to look after him as a father and compensate for what he failed to do to his father as a son. He referred to many books on astrology to learn how to determine and manipulate one's next birth. He is also very certain that he could succeed in his "project."

> He was confident he could succeed. He had never failed in his life, in anything he had begun. This was the most important and vital project he was working on. He did not needhelp or advice from any one. No one else on earth should know about his plan. He wasnot doing anything wrong. He was not committing any sin, against his father, against society or against himself. (*Moonstone*, 40)

Sandaruwan explored all the technological facilities including cloning to get his father as his child.

> There was no information available regarding cloned children. It had always been a very closely guarded secret by those who meddled with human cloning, claiming that the secrecy was in the best interest of the child. It was an accepted fact in the business world, if the right contacts, right place to look for information, and unlimited funds were available,

> nothing could be kept secret. Yet all his inquiries, official, unofficial, unethical and illegal still failed to provide any news of any cloned human child.
>
> He could have a child from his own cells. The doctors would still need an unfertilised eggfrom a woman, remove the nucleus from the egg, to be fused with Sandaruwan's cell, andthe resultant embryo to be implanted in a surrogate mother. Since it would be the DNA of Sandaruwan only, the child would be a replica of Sandaruwan but he will not be Sandaruwan. His life could not continue in the new life form, because his last thoughts could not be passed onto the child. (*Moonstone*, 53)

At last he decides to have a biological son for which he also chooses a bride from Sri Lanka. He has arranged a doctor who has a sufficient reserve of ova from the hosen girl. The doctor, as per Sandaruwan's plan, has to get the egg to be fertilized with Sandaruwan's sperm at the exact time as directed by Sandaruwan. He has come to Sri Lanka to kill his father at exactly the same time when the doctor will fertilize the egg with Sandaruwn's sperm.

Sandaruwan thought that he could manipulate birth and death just as he manipulated his business. He thought that he could rewrite Destiny with technology. But when he reaches home in Sri Lanka to see his father and kill him at the appointed hour, he finds him already dead. He comes to realise that Destiny has overtaken him and he cannot alter it. His overconfidence in his technological prowess gets shaken at its very roots. For the first time he realises that he has been defeated. Having realised the futility of wealth, power, and knowledge, he decides to renounce everything and disappear. The novel closes with the following lines that praise "Karma"

> The peaceful quiet world he had built up around himself collapsed like a pack of cards.
>
> *Anicca vata sankhara.* Everything in the world is impermanent. We live in an ever-changing world, while we ourselves are changing. We do not know what is in store for ustomorrow. (*Moonstone*, 117)

The novel is a brilliant example that depicts the hollowness of modern life. Life is meaningful only when it is lived. Life has to be experienced with its ups and downs and twists and turns. One cannot overpower the natural forces. One has to be ready to accept life as it comes. One must remember the lines of Tennyson in "Tithonus":

> Why should a man desire in any way
> To vary from the kindly race of men
> Or pass beyond the goal of ordinance
> Where all should pause, as is most meet for all? ("Tithonus")

Sandaruwan may be a fictitious character. But Daya Dissanayake, through his character, represents the pitiable modern man who suffers from an inward void that cannot be filled by money and power but only by spiritual pursuit.

Works Cited

Dissanayake, Daya. *Moonstone.* Sarasvi, 2006: Colombo.

CHAPTER 12

The Spiritual, Psychological, Philosophical, Scientific, Suspense Thriller Elements in Daya Dissanayake's *Moonstone*

R. Karthika Devi

Daya Dissanayake narrates the story of Sandaruwan in his three personalities or identities in the novel *Moonstone*. Sandaruwan takes three births or lives, according to his own ideology, at three different stages of life without sharing any common identity among the three – the first one as the poor son of Romiel, an agnostic Christian and a staunch Buddhist village girl Swarnalatha who was born and brought up in Amnagasthenna in Southern Sri Lanka; the second one as a billionaire owing an international level IT Business Empire; the third one as an enlightened but isolated being relinquishing all this belongings having realised the fact of life as a transient one.

The novel begins with Sandaruwan, the IT world billionaire returning to his home land Sri Lanka from the island mansion *Supaditi*, meaning well-suited, built in the Seychelles, which is an archipelago consisting of about one hundred and fifteen islands adorning the Indian Ocean with its coral reefs and rare fauna and flora. The author has vividly described why and how Sandaruwan has chosen the island for business network around the world. He was able to sit anywhere in the land, At first he thought of Sri Lanka for constructing a home for him, as he was unable to forget the serene beauty of his native soil with its beaches, the wilderness, the waterfalls and the birds. The cashew plantation in Eluwankulama on the western coast, the paddy field among the coconut, the neem and the banana trees situated near the mouth of the Kirindi Oya in the South, the jungle and the tea estate Nuwara Eliya with its waterfall, the tea estate on the border of Sinharaja and the virgin tropical forest lingered in his eyes. But, he negated them as the native locations might bring into light his past identity which he did not want to reveal to anybody as he considered his new life as Sandaruwan as an international business magnet as a new birth.

He pondered over various places in India such as Kerala, Karnataka, beach in Goa, place between Pune and Mumbai, Nasik and places in Himachal Pradesh. But, he gave up that too as he was afraid of the over-population and a number of languages. He considered Myanmar, Vietnam, Indonesia, Philippines and Thailand. At last, he chose the Seychelles which "was not in the path of the frequent helicopter flights" (21). He selected the name for his residence from the names of the Sri Lankan caves donated to the Buddhist monks. His choice of the location free from noise, dust and pollution reveals his aesthetic sense and his eco-consciousness. But, such an artistic oriented calm and quite soul came back to his home land with an idea of murdering his own father. And the novel begins with this knot which brings in the element of suspense thriller which makes the reader turn the pages fast to know further about Sanduruwan's life which moves backward to his earlier life as Chandraratne. The novel not only probes the external life of Chandraratne but also analyses the mind of Sandaruwan psychologically and discusses why he had decided to kill his father. In addition to describing the life of Chandraratne; the author also deals with the relationship between Chandraratne's father Romiel and his mother Swarnalatha. In fact, the novel moves chronologically backward increasing the curiosity of the reader and strengthening the suspense to know further, instead of revealing the past.

Swarnalatha was a Buddhist while Romiel was a Christian. Romiel originally belonged to Colombo and even there were gossips that he was not a Sinhala but a Tamil. Swarnalatha's father and uncle – Dhanasri and Gunasri had developed friendship with Romiel when they went to Colombo for selling their vegetables in the market. On the sudden demise of Dhanasri, Romiel voluntarily involved himself in the rituals and rites of his death and at that time itself the villagers had rumoured that Romiel had done all works not only for the friendship of Dhanasri but also for Swarnalatha. Later, he took care of Gunasri who was suffering from cancer. At last, the villagers accepted him as the husband of Swarnalatha. Yet, in the birth certificate of Chandraratne, for the question whether his father and mother were married, the answer was marked as 'No'. Moreover, Chandraratne too had a very dim remembrance of his mother. Her usual visit to the temple, her staunch faith in Buddhism and her white attire remained unforgotten in his heart. As usual, she was working in the vegetable plot one day. All of a sudden, she fell down and everyone shouted. His father brought her inside saying that she had been bitten by a snake. After her early death, Chandraratne as a very young child came directly under the control of his father.

Chandraratne's boyhood was not an interesting one because of the simplicity of a dull village life far away from the city where the comforts and the luxuries of life are adundant. But, Romiel talked to the headmaster of the town school and Chandraratne got the opportunity to go to study there. Though he thought of his father coming to the town school, he was actually happy that he did not come. Romiel would not wear any upper garment but only the loin cloth around his waist. He did not have the habit of wearing slippers too. In that condition, it was not possible for Chandraratne to show him as his father. Some students thought that the headmaster was the father and he did not take efforts to correct them. He was laughed at school for his long four word name which was a pride once in his school days in the village. The parents of town school parents were rich and came by car. During the holidays, these boys would go home. But Chandraratne avoided going home. In fact, for his inconveniences at school, he began to hate Romiel secretly. When he happened to go home, he alienated himself from his father and other village friends. The life in the village was boring to him. Yet, the author glorifies the whole village community as the larger extended family where there is no necessity of fences demarcating each one's property yet the unmarked boundaries were respected by each other.

But Chandraratne's hatred for his father is not a permanent one. He began to concentrate on his future, which, he had decided, should be a superior one. When he got distinction in the final examination, the principal asked him to serve as the maths teacher for grade VI and VIII. Though he had aspirations to go the university, he accepted the offer as it fulfilled his immediate need. Yet, he did not give up his efforts. He became a university lecturer with his intelligence coupled with his hard work. Here, the author takes diversion and deals with some of the postcolonial issues. Some people were in illusion that English was essential for progress in career. But, it is refuted by the author who mentions that there are some developed countries which use English only for international communication. Chandraratne had been popular among the girls during the university days because of his readiness to help them in their studies. For that, he was chased by other boys in order to get the votes of the girls in the university election. For his university education, Chandraratne, in addition to depending on the scholarship from the school and Mahapola Scholarship, did part time jobs such as programming. Thus, he stood as an example and a model for an ambitious student.

Being a son of the parents belonging to two different religions, his religious stance also remained a confusing one 'He did not consider himself as a Buddhist' (28). But, also, he says, 'I went to the temple, worshipped the Buddha statues, the Bodhi tree, the stupa, offered flowers' (28). He confirms saying, 'I don't follow any of these practices now, and I don't believe in such practices' (28). It involves a philosophical study and gives philosophical dimension to the novel.

In spite of his refusal to accept his religious stand, from the beginning till the end of the novel, the author mentions the Buddhist terms *Dhamma* and *Kamma* – the variations or the mutations of the Hindu *Dharma* and *Karma* in association with the life of Sandaruwan. Chandraratne got free Green card to go to his Los Angeles by lottery. At one stage, after entering IT world as the business magnet as the proprietor of thakshana.com at international level, Chandraratne decided to hide all his identity in his new world in terms of his name, native place, religion, nationality, caste, creed, etc. After a lot of speculation, he changed his name to Sandaruwan. He considered this transformation from Chandraratne of Sri Lanka to Sandaruwan as the billionaire of the global village as a new birth. He did not like but hated to be called "Sri Lankan Bill Gates". Being a computer wizard, he made everything and every work attractive, innovative and secretive. The employees received the highest salaries in his business concern. The parents nagged their children to work in thakshana.com. At one stage, after earning a few billions, his attraction towards money began to wane and he began to think of his father and how he had worked hard to look after him. The hatred inside him disappeared and immense love for father bloomed in his heart. In course of time, he could not think of anything except his father. There developed an inexpressible guilty consciousness in heart as he had not gone to see his father in his native place after getting employment in the university. During his work as the lecturer in the university, he used to send his father money orders which had not been encashed by him. After that, he stopped sending money. After entering the IT field, he did not find time to think of his native place and father. After enjoying all the luxuries of life, being single, not having any personal tie-up with any girl despite having moved with girls, he began to think of his father. His obsession with the thought of his father involves a deep psychological study. During his school days, the bitterness felt for his father was not actually hatred but the influence of the snobbery of the town boys. He had always recognised the sacrificial hard work of his father. He should have looked after him, when he had been able to stand on his own legs. But, at that time, his ambitious nature had not given him an opportunity to take care of his father. Now, he had realised that it was time for him to see him. He had wondered how people like Romiel lived without the comforts like fan and air-conditioner in their life. Now, he was able to provide everything to him. But, also, he could not expect to make his father accept what he would offer for his comfort as he had been accustomed to simplicity and there was no expectation in his father's heart to get anything from his son. But Sandaruwan desired that what all he had earned by him should be enjoyed by his father. With that intention, he has designed the first floor of his mansion Supaditi, despite knowing very well that his father would not need that. His heart was not ready to accept the truth. Nothing from his business empire could afford solace to his mind except fulfilling his filial duties despite Romiel's natural detachments from such expectation. He repeatedly pondered over how he could discharge his duties to him. All on a sudden, an idea flashed in his mind. He had decided that it would have been possible for him, if his father had been born to him as his son. This idea made him think over the concept of rebirth which gives a spiritual dimension to the novel. The idea of rebirth made Sandaruwan think philosophically:

> There are three root causes for the origination of kamma, greed, hatred and ignorance. An action done in greed, hate or ignorance wherever the individual is reborn, and wherever the action ripens, there are individual reaps the fruit of that action, be it in this life, in the next life or in future existences. That was what Sandaruwan had learnt as a child.
>
> No one can change the karmic effects or influence rebirth. Sandaruwan had boasted that he would never be born again, that he never had a previous life.
>
> Yet, with his study into rebirth, he slowly came to believe that death was not the complete annihilation of a being, and that it was only the

> cessation of a psycho-physical life of one existence, and that the karmic force remained undisturbed. He came to accept the Buddhist belief that rebirths occurred immediately instantaneously without going through any intermediate state *Antharabhava.* Immediately after the last moment of consciousness *Cuti citta,* there arises the relinking consciousness, *Pattisnadhi Vinjjana.* (105)

From the beginning Sandaruwan has been nowhere shown as thinking philosophically or religiously. As a boy, he was active and happy. He found his mother an ardent devotee of Buddha going to temples and worshipping the statues of Buddha. His father showed no interest either in Buddhism or in Christianity. Even after going to school or the university, he concentrated on his studies for a better future as he remained a butt of ridicule because of his rural background and poverty among the rich city boys. In his isolation, He seriously sought for materialistic prosperity with his higher education and job; He alienated himself from his poor, rustic father who seemed to be uninteresting to him and also from his village friends. When he won a lottery for free green card to go to U.S.A. he did not think of God. He becomes more vigorous to work for his materialistic progress. But in order to become the richest Asian business magnet, he further alienated from the world and his fellow beings. He was so careful that none should be able to know who he was. For that, he changed every one of his identities. And, he incarnated himself as Sandaruwan. His transformation from the poor, rural Chandraratne to the rich, multinational IT Corporate owner Sandaruwan actually did not give any solace or happiness to him but led to more isolation. He had designed his business empire in such a way that even without seeing and consulting him; the employees could proceed with their work at home and could be paid to their satisfaction. In fact, his thriving wealth in its saturation made him feel guilty consciousness. When he was suffering from poverty, he worked consciously without thinking anything except money. Now, the materialistic fulfilment offered him time to think of his father. He began to think how his father could live without any comforts of life. He visualised his father toiling in the field for the welfare of his son in the sun without wearing a shirt to cover his body or slippers to protect his feet. His obsession with his father made him think how he could serve his father to lead a cosy life. He knew very well that he would not come to his mansion "Supaditi". His repeated contemplation over his father convinced him to believe that only if his father was born as his own son, he could make use of his wealth for his father. Father in his condition would never accept anything from him as he was used to that way of life. So, Romiel should be born as son of Sandaruwan to enjoy his wealth. From that time onwards, Sandaruwan began to think in terms of soul and rebirth which have connection with *Karma* and religion. The Indian religions Hinduism and its offshoots Buddhism and Jainism believed in Karma and rebirth. Once he was satisfied with the argument over rebirth after analysing the concept religiously, he began to execute his mission scientifically. And, the novel takes a scientific turn.

Sandaruwan, being himself accustomed to the continuous victory in all his endeavours, was firm in his belief that it would be possible for him to make his father reborn as his own son. Rebirth is purely an Indian religious concept and as his mother had been a Buddhist, an Indian religion, he was able to follow it. Otherwise, had he been a Christian, he could not have thought of it. He began to analyse the possibilities of the rebirth of his father from different perspectives. He consulted the various websites in the internet. He thought of cloning. Cloning may be one of the easiest processes with which another living being as a same replica can be brought out. Yet, it would not be his son. If a cell or a DNA from any part of Romiel was taken and a new being was created, it would not be Sandaruan's son but only Sandaruwan's brother. Because, the new being would be the son of Romiel and Swarnalatha only. So, if Romiel had to be born as the son of Sandaruwan, he should die to be reborn as Sandaruwan's son on a particular time.

Sandaruwan once again involved in secret works for the rebirth of his father. He was in need of a surrogate mother to carry his sperm. He gave attractive advertisement for brides, not mentioning his real purpose. He chose the suitable woman and brought her to Sweden in order to collect her healthy ovum by an efficient obstetrician. He never revealed his identity to her. He spent a lot of money for her stay in Sweden and return to Sri Lanka. The obstetrician was well paid. He consulted the astrology. He calculated and worked out time and date for various activities associated with the rebirth of his father by referring to his birth date. At last he fixed the time and date for the death of his father to be reborn again.

Once again, as a postmodern alienated being, without revealing his identity and actually erasing his identity, he travelled to his father, who was living without any attention and without any expectation in a remote village, in order to kill him. In utter darkness, when he entered the hut of his father, to his dismay, he was found dead. He might have died two or three days earlier. He set fire in a calculative way so that it would fire ten minutes after his departure.

Now, he has become another living being. Sandaruwan seeking money and victory in business concerns died inside him. He was a new person to whom nothing was needed. He realised that nothing he possessed would have given pleasure or comfort to his father. In fact, he would not have been in need of him. Perhaps, he would never have expected him or anyone or anything in his life. This realisation changed the temperament of Sandruwan. Suddenly, he found emptiness in life. He felt nothingness in his victory. He felt neither hated nor love.

Sandaruwan, at once, relinquished everything. He left his car and money as they were. Without any destination, he took the bus going to Anurathapuram. On the way, the bus stopped. He got down and found a charity home for the aged run by the Christian missionary. At first, the sisters did not believe him. But, his commitment and dedication to the old people really pleased them. He believed that he served the poor old people what he could not do for his own father.

Sandaruwan actually had programmed everything for the running of his business concern and the birth and the brought up of the child born out of the ovum collected from the surrogate mother in Sweden and his own sperm. But in his frustration over his father's death he had forgotten to calculate the time and the date for the birth of the child. According to astrology, it would be a boy. He had already given the child a name, 'Omri', as it is close to his own father's name.

At last, Sandaruwan thought of other possibilities. He thought over the question what would happen to Omri, if Omri also, in future, likes to see his own father as Sandaruwan did, and if Sandaruwan declines his son Omri's request to go back to the city. The question demolished the entire 'peaceful world' (112) he had constructed.

To Sandaruwan, everything in the world looked impermanent, *Anicca Vata Sankhara*. The author concludes the novel with the Buddhist idea of the world as *maya* and refers to the eternally changing nature of the world. He has aptly given the last chapter the title 'Wheel' which symbolises the very nature of human life.

Works Cited

Dissanayake, Daya. *Moonstone.* e-novel, 2006.

Bio-notes of Contributors

1. **Dr. S. Karthik Kumar** is a faculty at the Department of English, Annamalai University, Tamil Nadu, India. He has been teaching literature, criticism, and theory for more than twenty years in the ninety-year old department. He has published articles and chapters in books on a range of titles. He has authored two books and edited four books. He has been as resource person for several seminars, conferences, workshops, etc. For his doctoral degree, he has specialised in Postcolonial literature. His research interest lies in Eco-criticism and Indigenous narratives.
2. **Dr. Anita Arul X.** is an assistant professor in English in the Department of English, Pasumpon Muthuramalinga Thevar College, Melaneelithanallur, Sankarankovil. She lives at Tenkasi, Tenkasi District, Tamilnadu, India. She is handling English to Under Graduate students. Her research interests are mainly on Indian post-colonial literature. A critic, she has some good number of papers to her credit. She has research publications at National, International level journals and anthologies, and presented papers in seminars and conferences. She has been a resource person to various colleges. She is also a research supervisor under the jurisdiction of Manonmaniam Sundaranar University, Tirunelveli, Tamilnadu, India.
3. **Dr. R. Karthika Devi**, Assistant Professor of English, M.V.Muthaiah Government Arts College for Women, Dindigul, Tamil Nadu, presented papers in 42 national and international conferences. She has published Research articles in journals and edited volumes. She regularly contributes to journals and volumes. A total of 26 M. Phil. Scholars have completed their dissertation under her guidance. Four candidates are currently doing PhD under her guidance.
4. **Dr. G. Srilatha** is Associate Professor and Head, Department of English, PB Siddhartha College of Arts and Science, Vijayawada (A.P). She has organised various Seminars and Conferences. She

has published many research articles in Journals and books. Her areas of special interest include American Literature, Indian Literature and Aboriginal Studies.

5. **Mrs. S. Malathy**, Assistant professor, Tagore Arts College, Puducherry, is a senior faculty with well over two decades of teaching experience. She has paper publications in national and international journals besides innumerable book chapters in volumes. Over a period of time, she has established herself as a critic in Literature.

6. **Dr. Palakurthy Dinakar** teaches English at Government Degree College, Huzurabad, Dist: Karimnagar of Telangana state. He has 24 years of experience in teaching English language and literature at various levels. He received Gold Medal in MA English and first rank in MPhil and did his Ph.D. in Translation Studies from Kakatiya University. He has P.G.D.T.E. from EFLU (English and Foreign Languages University), Hyderabad. He was the first ranker among the south Indian participants in Teacher Development programme conducted by Regional Institute of English, South India, Bangalore. He presented research papers in 8 International, 35 National Seminars and attended 20 Webinars. He published 70 research articles in edited anthologies and scholarly journals. He translated more than 100 poems and 50 short stories from Telugu to English out of which several were published. His translated poetry was published in Central Sahitya Akademi's Indian Literature, Telangana Sahitya Akademi's '*Parampara*' and Dept. Of Language and Culture, Telangana State's 'Green Garland'. His translated short stories were published in Central Sahitya Akademi's 'Beyond the Backyard, 'Telangana Sahitya Akademi's '*Asthitwa*' and Dept. Of Language and Culture, Telangana State's 'Telangana Harvest' and also in journals like Kakatiya Journal of English Studies, Langlit, *Guduvari, Madhuravani*and *Mayukha* His other translated stories were published in 'Essence of Life' and 'Intimacies'. His recent translation of P.V. Narasimha Rao's novella 'Mangayya's Fortune' attracted considerable critical acclaim from literary circles. He authored 15 books on English Language and Pedagogy among them *Proficiency in English, Reading and Reflecting on Texts* and *Teaching English through Discourse Oriented Pedagogy* are well known. He is the content developer for UG I & II Year courses of

Kakatiya and Satavahana Universities namely *English for Enrichment* (Oxford University Press), English for Accomplishment (Cambridge University Press) and *English for Communication* –1 (Cambridge University Press) for Satavahana University. He edited 06 books on Language and Literary criticism. His *Poetry to Politics: Tributes to Sri. P.V. Narasimha Rao* and *Teaching English: Practices, Problems & Principles* are widely read. He gave more than 60 extension lectures offline and online on Communication and Soft Skills across the state. His speeches were broadcast from All India Radio, Hyderabad and Warangal stations. He received best teacher awards from the state government, teacher organisation and NGOs. Recently *Anuvada Adithya* awardhas been conferred on him by Sarvaardha Samkshema Samithi, Hyderabad.

7. **Mrs. Renu Milind Dhotre**, Research Scholar, University of Mumbai. A veteran teacher, she has twenty years of teaching experience as teacher of English. She has paper publications and paper presentations to her credit. She is actively engaged in Language Teaching though literature is her primary interest.

8. **Dr. D. Vijaya Lakshmi** has been working as an Associate Professor in Sri Vishnu Educational Society since 2004. Her academic progress and research pursuit enabled her to enter the research arena nearly from two decades. She is fortune enough to contribute her ideas in various national and international conferences, seminars and workshops. As an academician she believes that her learning, pursuits are eternal and she endorses holistic approach in all walks of life. Holding various responsibilities, both academic and administrative, she fine-tuned her skills. Catering to the present needs of the students and the industry, she succeeded in creating a strategic system of training to the students for their placements, soft skills, personality development, and so on by implementing innovative approaches in teaching learning process.

9. **Dr.N. U. Lekshmi**, Assistant Professor of English and Research Supervisor has carved a space in the field of education since fifteen years. She is a commendable academician with a MA MEd PhD NET in English and NET in Education. In addition to being a vibrant resource person, she has organised several international and national seminars, published several volumes of

edited books, and has to her credit articles and poems published in reputed books and journals. She has received recognition including the award as the Programme Officer of the best NSS Unit. Her areas of interest include English Language Teaching, Translation Studies and Critical Theories.

10. **S.P. Soubhagya**, Assistant Professor of English is interested in research and is an upcoming writer. She has a brilliant academic career and has published various research articles in national as well as international journals. Creative writing is one of her favorite fields.
11. **Dr. Anju S. Nair** has presented a number of research articles in national and international Seminars. She has publications in national and international journals and books. Is interested in critical theory. Is working as an Assistant professor of English at Tagore Govt Arts and Science College, Pondicherry.
12. **Dr. Lily Arul Sharmila** was a student of Madras Christian College, Chennai presently she is a faculty of English, Tagore Government Arts and Science College, Puducherry. She is a passionate propagator of students' empowerment through learning as she hails from the teacher's family. She spreads the message, content and knowledge by carrying out her roles and demands as a long standing professional with exemplary dedication and extraordinary humility. She has more than two decades of her meritorious services. Her research papers are an offshoot of her insatiable appetite and thirst for knowledge in academic front. She has attended more than 50 seminars and written more than 75 research papers under the academic integrity and climate. She vows to continue her research contributions with her robust, sound and rational attitudes. Her living ethics are to illumine the minds and transpire the hearts with unique combinations of pristine aura and sublime strings of efforts.
13. **Dr. M. Beula Hemalatha** serves as an Assistant Professor of English in Nazareth Margoschis College, Pillaiyanmanai, Toothkudi Dist, Tamil Nadu. She has fourteen years of experience in teaching, research and administration. She has good exposure and experience in extension services.

Her major areas of research include Diasporic Studies, Jewish Literature. She is a research Supervisor of Manonmaniam Sundarnar University and a member of ALAPAN.

14. **Miss J. Miraclin** is an Undergraduate Student in the Research Department of English, Nazareth Margoschis College Pillaiyanmanai. Her area of interest is Post-Colonial Literature. Her fervent interest in on Euthenics impelled to contribute a research paper.

Editor's Bio-note

P.V. Laxmiprasad, M.A. PhD is an eminent academician, an erudite scholar, a literary critic, a resource person and a senior editor. He has so far published 36 books in English literature. Basically, his area of research interest is *Literary Criticism.* Besides, he has to his credit 70 research papers, 120 poems, 55 book reviews, a few translations and held interviews with literary legends. He has published research papers in UGC Care Enlisted and foreign journals. All his publications speak of outstanding credentials and long standing contribution to literature. His research interests include Indian Writing in English, English language Teaching and Literary Criticism. Overall, he has 300 publications to his credit. He has a strong passion for literature and music. Currently, he is teaching in the Department of English, Satavahana University, Karimnagar, Telangana.

Contact details: 07989446153

Mail Id: laxmiprasad.puram@gmail.com

Book Publications

Books 37

I: Authored Books (Literary Criticism)

1. The Mirror and the Light: Critical Essays on Indian Writing in English (Aadi Publications, Jaipur, India. 2021) ISBN: 978-93-87799-59-2
2. Swami Paramananda's The Upanishads: A Study of Eternal Sparks: HSRA Publishers, Bangalore, India. 2021. ISBN:
3. S. Radhakrishnan's The Hindu View of Life: A Study of Cultural Touchstones. The Impish Lass Publishing House, Mumbai.2021.ISBN: 978-81-950910-5-8
4. Tagore as Philosophical Voyager: A Critical Study of Gitanjali. Academica Press, Washington, USA.2021.ISBN: 978-1-68053-937-0

5. Quotes Quotable: Critical Responses to Jiddu Krishnamurti's Quotes, Authorspress, New Delhi, 2021 ISBN: 978-93-90588-44-2
6. Thiruvalluar's Kural: A Scholarly Review. HSRA Press, Bengaluru, 2021
7. Kahlil Gibran's The Prophet: A Study of Philosophic Profundities. Authors Press, New Delhi. 2021 ISBN: 978-93-90891-50-4
8. The Philosophy of Bhagavadgita. Booksclinic Publishing, Bilaspur, 2021. ISBN: 978-93-5535-090-9
9. The Holocaust of Partition: A Study of Saadat Hasan Manto's Mottled Dawn, Authors Press, New Delhi, 2021.ISBN: 978-93-90891-45-0
10. The Quintessence of Quotes and Speeches: A Study of Swami Vivekannada's Thoughts to Inspire and 25 Greatest Speeches, Nitya Publications, Bhopal, India, 2021. ISBN: 978-93-91257-66-8
11. Mahasweta Devi's The Queen of Jhansi – A Subaltern Study – HSRA Press, Bengaluru 2021. ISBN: 978-93-90903-40-5.
12. Sita – Living Indian Psyche: A Critical Study of Chitra Banerjee Divakaruni's The Forest of Enchantments, Nitya Publications, Bhopal, 2021 ISBN:978-93-91257-56-9
13. Contextualising Woman and Her Struggles: A Critical Study of Indira Goswami's Five Novellas about Women, Book River Press, India, 2021. ISBN:
14. Rewriting Indian History: Colonial Encounters in Chitra Banerjee Divakaruni's The Last Queen and Basavaraj Naikar's The Queen of Kittur, Academica Press, Washington, USA, 2021. ISBN: 9781680532524
15. The Artist and the Artistry: Critical Essays on Indian Writing in English (BFC Publications, Lucknow, 2020) ISBN: 978-93-90478-63-7
16. Indian Images in the Select Novels of Paul Scott, Authorspress, New Delhi, 2018 ISBN: 978-93-87651-28-9
17. The Philosophical Muse: Perspectives on the Poetry of K.V. Raghupathi ISBN: 978-93-313-1804-6, APH Publishing Corporation, New Delhi, 2012

II: Edited Volumes (Criticism)

1. Bridges across the Nation: The Vitality of Indian Literatures in English Translation, Authors press, New Delhi, 2021. ISBN: 978-93-91314-46-0
2. The Mirror and the Reflections: Interpreting Literatures through Literary Theories, Academica Press, Washington – London, 2020 ISBN: 978-16-8053-0975
3. Contours of Shiv K Kumar's Poetry: Relocation and Rediscovery. Authors Press New Delhi. 2019 ISBN: 978-93-89625-24-1
4. The Heterogeneity of Story Writing: A Critical Evaluation of Eight Indian Short Story writers in English, Authors Press, 2015 ISBN: 978-93-5207-038-1.
5. Critical Readings on the Fictional World of Manju Kapur, Aadi Publications, Jaipur, 2016 ISBN: 978-93-82630-88-3.
6. Living through Mahesh Dattani's Plays, Authors Press, New Delhi, 2018. ISBN: 978-93-88008-19-83
7. The Writings of Amitav Ghosh: Exploration of Multiple Worlds, Atlantic Publishers. ISBN:
8. 978-81-269-2943-6.
9. Imprisonment as Creative Art: A Critical Study of Prison Writings, Authors Press, New Delhi, 2021 ISBN: 978-93-90588-90-9
10. An Anthology of Criticism on Six Indian English Poets, Sarup Publications 2015, New Delhi ISBN: 978-81-7625-987-3.
11. Mapping Thematic Variations: The Poetry of DC Chambial, Authors Press 2015, New Delhi ISBN: 978-93-5207-022-0.
12. The Spirit of Age and Ideas in the Novels of PCK Prem, Authors Press, New Delhi ISBN: 978-93-5207-414-3
13. The Poetry of I. K. Sharma: New Tracks and Literary Swings, Authors Press, New Delhi,2017, ISBN 978-93-5207-554-6
14. Exploring New Horizons: Myriad Dimensions in the Poetry of Manas Bakshi. Authorspress, New Delhi, 2017. ISBN: 978-93-86722-65-2
15. The Nativist Vision of Life in the Works of BasavarajNaikar, Authors Press, New Delhi, 2018. ISBN: 978-93-87781-55-4

16. The Poetry of T.V. Reddy: A Critical Study of Humanistic Concerns, MHP, Michigan, USA, 2018. 978-1-61599-371-0
17. Critical Spectrum: The Short Stories of P. Raja, Authorspress, New Delhi, 2018. ISBN: 978-93-87281-91-2
18. The Poetry of Raama Chandramouli: Critical Perspectives. Reliance Publishing House, New Delhi. 2019. ISBN: 978-81-7510-253-8
19. Introspective Voyager: A Collection of Critical Essays on the Poetry of K.V.Raghupathi, Authors Press, 2014. New Delhi ISBN: 978-81-7273-850-1.

Creative Works

1. From Epidemic to Pandemic: A Memoir of Covid-19 (Upcoming)
2. Universal Witness – Poetry Collection in English, ISBN: 978-81-921073-7-0 Thematics Publication, Latur, M.S. 2012.

Index